th
PRAYER
we
OFFER

A Catholic Guide
to Communion with God

P E T E R J.
VAGHI

foreword by
Cardinal Seán O'Malley, O.F.M. Cap.

ave maria press AmP notre dame, indiana

Nihil Obstat: Reverend Monsignor Michael Heintz, PhD
                  Censor Librorum

Imprimatur: Most Reverend Kevin C. Rhoades
                  Bishop of Fort Wayne–South Bend

                  Given at: Fort Wayne, Indiana, on 19 September 2011

Founded in 1865, Ave Maria Press is a ministry of the United States Province of Holy Cross.

www.avemariapress.com

ISBN-10 1-59471-294-8 ISBN-13 978-1-59471-294-4

Cover image ©Thinkstock.

Cover and text design by David Scholtes.

Printed and bound in the United States of America.

Library of Congress Cataloging-in-Publication Data
Vaghi, Peter J.
  The prayer we offer : a Catholic guide to communion with God / Peter J. Vaghi.
      p. cm. -- (The pillars of faith series)
  Includes bibliographical references and index.
   ISBN 978-1-59471-294-4 (pbk. : alk. paper) -- ISBN 1-59471-294-8 (pbk. : alk. paper)
  1. Prayer--Catholic Church. 2. Prayer--Christianity. 3. Catholic Church--Doctrines. 4. Spiritual life--Catholic Church. I. Title.
  BV210.3.V34 2012
  48.3'2--dc23

                              2011045511

the PRAYER *we* OFFER

"In concluding his four volume series, it is fitting that this book provides such rich and nourishing insight into the challenge to every believer to pray always and, in doing so, to lift our hearts and minds to God."

Cardinal Donald Wuerl
Archbishop of Washington

"A treasure that renders a great service to those learning about prayer, those who guide them, and those who would like a comprehensive survey of Catholic teaching and traditions of prayer. Guiding our walk with God, *The Prayer We Offer* will become a textbook for seminarians, RCIA candidates, and students of authentic Catholic piety."

Archbishop Timothy P. Broglio
Archbishop for the Military Services, USA

"I highly recommend *The Prayer We Offer* to all who seek a deep, personal encounter with the Lord Jesus in the community of the Church."

Rev. Thomas Rosica, C.S.B.
CEO
Salt and Light Catholic Media Foundation

"Msgr. Vaghi writes as a true pastor teaching his people to pray—and us as well. If you are looking for an inspiring and accessible guide to prayer, *The Prayer We Offer* is the place to go."

Rev. Alfred McBride, O. Praem.
Author of *Staying Faithful Today*

"In *The Prayer We Offer*, Msgr. Peter Vaghi invites us to delve more deeply into the fourth and most beautiful section of *The Catechism of the Catholic Church*. With its practical wisdom and reflective questions, this book will help many to embrace the call to 'pray always.'"

Donna Orsuto
Pontifical Gregorian University
Director, The Lay Centre at Foyer Unitas

"Msgr. Vaghi has performed a genuine service in this book. *The Prayer We Offer* provides us with encouragement and guidance in coming to an experiential knowledge of the realities the Catechism teaches. This is a valuable contribution to Catholic spirituality."

Rev. Francis Martin
Professor Emeritus
Dominican House of Studies

Dedicated to the memory of Archbishop Pietro Sambi, Apostolic Nuncio to the United States from 2006 to 2011.

I am personally deeply grateful for his support of this Pillars of Faith series which he referred to as a "praiseworthy endeavor." As an honorary member of the John Carroll Society and a faithful friend to the parish of the Little Flower in Bethesda, Maryland, he will be greatly missed. May he rest in peace! Special gratitude to the parishioners of Little Flower Parish and members of the John Carroll Society; to my editor, Robert Hamma; and to Gerald O'Collins, S.J., Father Anthony Lickteig, Stephen Koeth, C.S.C., Adoreen McCormick, and Robert Boxie.

The Pillars of Faith Series
by Msgr Peter J. Vaghi

The Faith We Profess:
A Catholic Guide to the Apostles' Creed

The Sacraments We Celebrate:
A Catholic Guide to the Seven Mysteries of Faith

The Commandments We Keep:
A Catholic Guide to Living a Moral Life

The Prayer We Offer:
A Catholic Guide to Communion with God

Contents

Foreword

The Church's mission of evangelizing, of fulfilling the great commission to make disciples of all nations, begins at Pentecost. Pentecost itself is a sort of paradigm for the Church. In a moment of crisis, fear, and of confusion the Church came together to pray, gathered at the place of the first Eucharist, in the company of Mary, Peter, and the Apostles. Their prayer opened their hearts to the Spirit who energized them to go out and share what they had received.

Today, passing on the faith must take place in a Pentecost experience. It begins with intense communal prayer—in the company of Mary, the Mother of God, and with the ministry of Peter and the apostolic college. We need to teach people, especially children and young people, how to pray. This book is an important resource for the contemporary Catholic community and for those who seek to learn more about our faith. We need to be people of prayer and teachers of prayer. It is impossible to pass on the faith without forming people in the life of prayer. Faith without prayer is a contradiction; it is information, it is doctrine, it is history, but it is not faith. Prayer and worship are the paths of discipleship. As Msgr. Vaghi shares in the first chapter of this final volume of the Pillars of Faith series, prayer is indeed God's gift and initiative in our lives.

Evangelization is the mission of the Church, which is itself an extension of Jesus Christ who is the *Magister*, the Teacher. He wants to communicate to us life in abundance. The mission of the Church is about making disciples, helping people respond to the call to holiness by being part of a faith-filled, worshipping community that comes together in prayer, striving to follow Jesus' teaching and example.

This is not something new in the history of the Church. One of the first attempts is documented in the first century *Didache*, the Church's first training manual for initiating people into the Church's life and worship. It was memorized by teachers who used it as a lesson plan, catechism, liturgical worship aide, and a primer for faithful discipleship.

The Prayer We Offer is a kind of *Didache* for the twenty-first century, initiating readers into the Church's life of prayer in all its forms. Msgr. Vaghi draws skillfully on his extensive experience as a pastor and teacher to help readers come to a new appreciation of prayer—first and foremost in the Eucharist, but also prayer in all the rich communal and personal expressions that our Catholic faith offers us.

It is challenging to be a teacher of prayer in our culture, to help young Catholics experience prayer so that when they gather for the Sunday Eucharist, they have a notion of why they are there and how to pray. But there can be no Catholic life, no holiness or discipleship without prayer. It is my hope that this book will help you gain a better understanding of the foundations of prayer in the Church and the practical means of incorporating prayer into the full range of one's life experiences. We are greatly blessed that Msgr. Vaghi has generously given of his time, his skill, and his prayer to provide us this guide.

Cardinal Seán O'Malley, O.F.M. Cap.
Archbishop of Boston

Preface

Saint Luke recounts in his gospel that Jesus told his disciples "a parable about the necessity for them to pray always without becoming weary" (Lk 18:1). Perhaps the reason Jesus needed to use a story to get his point across was because even the apostles found it difficult to understand what prayer was and how it should be such an all-inclusive part of daily life. Earlier in that same Gospel, the apostles asked Jesus: "Lord, teach us to pray" (Lk 11:1). The questions that the apostles asked in the context of Jesus' expectation of them are questions we ask today. One reason we inquire about how we are to pray is because as followers of Jesus we should accept his recommendation that we "pray always." We turn then to Christ's Church for the understanding of how we are to pray and in what sense it can be said that we are to pray always.

As he has done throughout all of his catechetical expositions of the faith of the Church, Msgr. Peter J. Vaghi, in *The Prayer We Offer*, helps us along the way as we try to grow more deeply in the Church's understanding of prayer, how we pray, and why we should pray. This is the final book in a series entitled Pillars of Faith, and it addresses the last of the four pillars of the *Catechism of the Catholic Church.*

Christ is the model and teacher of prayer. A person who faithfully embraces Jesus will necessarily devote careful attention to the Master's pattern of living as well as to his teaching. Both the lifestyle and the words of Jesus show that prayer should have an important place in the life of every Christian.

Among the answers to the question "What is prayer?" is the definition offered by St. John Damascene: "Prayer is the raising of one's mind and heart to God for the requesting of good things from God" (cf. *CCC* 257). This traditional definition has endured so long because it sums up what is an otherwise complex and multifaceted activity. The verb *to pray* means, simply, to ask for something. Yet prayer is much more than just asking God for a specific response. Our understanding of prayer needs to include that it is more than an activity of the intellect. A person's will, affections, and activities are all to be lifted up to God, to enter a true personal relationship with him.

Msgr. Vaghi's volume is so valuable because it walks the reader through the many examples of prayer and presents a variety of models of prayer. In the opening portions of his book, he speaks about prayer as God's gift, Old Testament models of prayer and, finally, Jesus as the master of prayer. Then he moves us into the wealth of manifestations of prayer. Here we are introduced to reflections on "the words from the cross" and, of course, the Church's great chain of prayers, the Rosary.

First and foremost among the many manifestations of the Church's prayer is the Lord's Prayer. Thus, Msgr. Vaghi directs considerable attention to the prayer of Jesus and its meaning. The Church celebrates this prayer as her most cherished one. She gives it a central place at Mass and in her liturgical worship and commends it to all. In this prayer that has been called "a summary of the whole Gospel," Christ teaches us two things: the spirit in which we should pray and the things for which we must ask.

As we come to reflect more deeply on prayer in the life of the Church, we understand, as *The Prayer We Offer* points out, prayer is more than an exercise of the mind. It involves a genuflection of the will to God. Genuine devotion should not be confused with feeling satisfaction or even good emotions. True devotion is properly directed to God. At times, our prayers may result in a sense of joy, personal peace, or even satisfaction. But such a response is not the gauge of the effectiveness of our prayer life. It is God to whom we speak and who makes up the other side of the conversation. His response may involve us in something far more profound than fleeting feeling.

Over his years as a pastor and teacher, Msgr. Vaghi has developed great skills, all of which he brings to bear in this volume. In concluding his four volume series, it is fitting that this book provides such rich and nourishing insight into the challenge to every believer to pray always and, in doing so, to lift our hearts and minds to God.

Donald Cardinal Wuerl
Archbishop of Washington

Introduction

This is the fourth and final book in the series entitled Pillars of Faith. It treats the last section of the *Catechism of the Catholic Church*, the last of the four pillars of the Catechism. While prayer may be the last section of the Catechism, it is certainly not incidental to our faith. As Jesuit Father Gerald O'Collins aptly writes:

> Prayer is not an accessory, not even a valuable accessory, to Christian life—something added on to make a better Christian out of a good one. Right from the New Testament times, a follower of Jesus has been understood to be someone who gives regular time to prayer. The very first Christian letter that has survived insists: ". . . pray continually. Give thanks whatever happens; for this is what God wills for you in Christ Jesus." (1 Thes 5:17–18)

The other books in this series address our faith professed (*The Faith We Profess: A Catholic Guide to the Apostles' Creed*), celebrated (*The Sacraments We Celebrate: A Catholic Guide to the Seven Mysteries of Faith*), and lived (*The Commandments We Keep: A Catholic Guide to Living a Moral Life*). In the Creed, we confess the wonderful things our God has done for us, especially sending his Son Jesus to be our savior and redeemer. The sacraments, our encounters with the living Lord, are the

privileged means by which our God continues to give
his new life to us in our day, and strengthens and devel-
ops that new life within us. That same faith which we
confess calls us, in the third part of the Catechism, to
lead a life worthy of our new-found dignity made possible by our Baptism into Christ Jesus. It is a life "worthy of the gospel of Christ" (Phil 1:27). Christians are
called to be imitators of Christ, to live *in* Christ. As St.
Paul reminds us in his letter to the Galatians, "I have
been crucified with Christ; yet I live, no longer I, but
Christ lives *in* me," (Gal 2:19–20), or as he writes in
2 Corinthians: "So whoever is in Christ is a new creation" (5:17). Still further St. Paul writes: "Incorporated
into *Christ* by Baptism, Christians are 'dead to sin and
alive to God in Christ Jesus'" (CCC 1694).

The last section of the *Catechism of the Catholic
Church*, the shortest by far at only seventy-five pages in
the English edition, explains the meaning and importance of prayer in the life of those of us who are believers and called to be followers of Jesus. Prayer is so
important—indeed essential—to our spiritual lives.
It is a beautiful part of the Catechism. This book is
designed to help feed our prayer lives, to help us grow
in prayer, and come to a deeper understanding of
prayer. It is not meant simply to be an academic exercise, but an effort to expand our relationship with God
in prayer.

Our subject matter in this book includes an expanded commentary on the Lord's Prayer—referred to by
Tertullian as "the summary of the whole Gospel" (CCC
2761). It also includes a reflection on Mary's prayer,
the holy Rosary. It is an expanded treatise on the very
nature of prayer itself. Emphasis is on the universal

call of all to pray: prayer in the Old Testament, the prayer of Jesus who is the master of prayer, the varieties of prayer, the liturgical tradition of prayer, prayer and the Trinity, and the various teachers of prayer. Another section deals with the vocal, meditative, and contemplative prayer, the difficulties of praying, and the efficacy of prayer. We will also reflect on the great final prayers of Jesus: his "farewell prayer" at the Last Supper, his prayer at Gethsemane, and his prayer from the wood of the cross.

Throughout this final section of the Catechism on prayer, there are numerous cross-references in the margin of the text (italicized numbers referring to other paragraphs within the Catechism that deal with the same theme). I encourage you to read the Catechism and to refer to these cross-references. In this way you will truly appreciate the organic presentation of the faith and its relationship to our lives of prayer.

As with the other books in the Pillars of Faith series, there are reflection questions and a prayer after each chapter. At the end of each chapter, there is also a witness statement from various contributors about their own prayer lives. These resources enable a small group to gather to reflect together on their faith. The prayer provided, or any familiar prayer, hymn, or psalm may be used to open and/or conclude each gathering. Of course, these resources may also be used personally to reflect and pray as one proceeds through this process.

The nine chapters of this book draw from the great tradition of our Catholic faith as expressed in the universal *Catechism of the Catholic Church* (CCC) and the *United States Catholic Catechism for Adults* (USCCA). This book also examines prayer through the prism of the writings of our late Holy Father, Blessed John Paul II, and of Pope Benedict XVI. References in the text to the *Catechism of the Catholic Church* are accompanied by the paragraph number, for example (*CCC* 572). References to the *United States Catholic Catechism for Adults* are given by the page number, for example (*USCCA* 165).

Throughout the book you will find references to the writings of Blessed John Paul II, Pope Benedict XVI, other popes, theologians, and writers, as well as the documents of the Second Vatican Council. These documents are referred to by their English names, often accompanied by their corresponding Latin titles, and referenced by the Latin titles' abbreviations. For example, Pope Benedict XVI's encyclical, *Saved by Hope,* is referenced as *SS* for its Latin title, *Spe Salvi,* followed by the paragraph number. (Abbreviations are listed on page 133.) With the exception of the documents of the Second Vatican Council, which are quoted from the edition edited by Austin Flannery, all other Church documents quoted in this book are taken from the Vatican website (www.vatican.va). The site has an excellent search engine. For the most efficient search results, enter the Latin name of the document. When quotations are taken from addresses by the Holy Father, these are noted by date. The full text of these addresses can be found by searching the Vatican website by date. Other sources quoted are referenced at the end of the book. These citations are arranged by chapter in the order in which they appear.

Pope Benedict XVI, in an Easter Monday talk, spoke of the enduring challenge to be an Easter witness and how this relates to prayer. He raises the question:

How can we encounter the Lord and increasingly become his authentic witnesses? St. Maximus of Turin stated: "Anyone who wishes to reach the Saviour must first, in his own faith, seat him at the right hand of the Divinity, and place him with heartfelt conviction in Heaven" (*Sermon 39* a, 3: *CCL* 23, 157), in other words one must learn to focus the gaze of one's mind and heart constantly on the heights of God, where the Risen Christ is. In this way God encounters man in prayer and adoration. . . . Only if we are able to turn to God, to pray to him, do we discover the deepest meaning of our life and the daily routine is illumined by the light of the Risen One. (Angelus, April 25, 2011)

At the basis of the Catechism, the *great* unifier is Jesus Christ. It is Jesus Christ, the teacher, who illuminates and sustains these four pillars of our Christian existence—faith, liturgy, morality, and prayer. In his very person, he is, after all, the object and subject of the true faith. He is present with his saving action in the Church and in her sacraments. He is the model, source, and support, with his grace, of Christian action. And together with the Holy Spirit, he is the teacher and inspiration of our prayer to the Father.

one

Prayer, God's Gift
and Initiative in Our Lives

Prayer, as Blessed John Paul II taught us, is the breath of the Holy Spirit. Archbishop Fulton J. Sheen used to say that his daily hour of prayer before the Blessed Sacrament was like "an oxygen tank that revived the breath of the Holy Spirit" (*USCCA* 461). St. Thérèse of Lisieux writes: "For me, prayer is a surge of the heart; it is a simple look turned toward heaven, it is a cry of recognition and of love, embracing both trial and joy" (*CCC* 2558). At its foundation, however, the desire for God of each one of us, a desire written on the human heart, is expressed and experienced in different ways. And we call it prayer. Moreover, we are challenged by St. Paul to pray constantly, yet so many things come between us and the voice of God. Our God so desires to spend time with us, to speak to us, to listen to us. And he really listens to us.

Prayer is important—indeed essential—to our spiritual lives, to growth in our spiritual lives. Ghanaian Cardinal Peter Turkson, President of the Pontifical Council for Justice and Peace, said: "I think the basis of any Christian spiritual growth is prayer and the Word of God. When these two things are not there, we are not connected to Jesus, and without him we can do nothing."

We are all on a journey of prayer and, undoubtedly, each of us seeks and desires to grow in prayer,
to find a special out-of-the-way place where we regularly meet Jesus, and to make prayer a continual part
of our daily lives. But oh, the challenges that we face
in our efforts to cultivate a life of prayer! They are not
foreign to me. My daily struggle begins as soon as I
awake each morning. Do I turn on the computer to
check my e-mail or do I open my breviary and dedicate
that time in the early hours of the morning—fresh and
good time—to God? At the break of dawn, do I pray
that beautiful line from Psalm 55: "O God, listen to my
prayer, do not hide from my pleading, attend to me
and reply"? Or are the headlines of the paper seemingly more important? It is at that very moment that I
must make a choice. How I resolve that choice surely
affects the rest of my day. Each of us has a similar challenge as we seek to follow and find the Lord Jesus and
make him central to our lives.

Christian life, of necessity, is marked by much out-
ward activity and a corresponding need for regular
inner retreat. We need a time and a place to wrestle
with our own hearts before God. Without this inner
retreat, the Christian life runs the risk of being simply
a facade. Too much activity without reflection can also
lead to burnout. A lack of spiritual nourishment leaves
us directionless, helpless, and very vulnerable to the
seductions and attacks of the evil one.

It is always difficult to find quiet time for God in
prayer. But how rewarding it is once it becomes a part
of our daily routine! It has changed my life as a priest.
After much struggle and experimentation, I have finally settled on the early hours of the morning as the best

time to pray—before all the normal demands of an active day intrude. What is the best time in your daily schedule for you to pray? It might take some experimentation, but once you have figured it out, your life will never be the same. I can attest to that.

We know from the gospel accounts that even Jesus was challenged to find a place for quiet prayer. He routinely went off to the desert to pray, and especially took time to commune with his Father before every major decision in his life. It was a struggle for him to find this space and time. Jesus' own struggle in this area should instruct each of us, his followers, and encourage us in our efforts.

The Gift of God

Jesus tells us so much about prayer in the gospels. I would like to focus on just one passage that is not often considered as a passage about prayer, the story of the Samaritan woman at the well (Jn 4:4–15). Jesus, on a journey passing through Samaria, was tired and sat down by a well, Jacob's well. It was like an oasis in the desert. So often each of us is tired from the deadlines of life, from the pressures of work, and each of us looks for an oasis in our own lives, somewhere to get away to in order to be refreshed, a quiet place. Certainly that was Jesus' intent. But what happens? Almost immediately, Jesus is interrupted. He encounters a woman, an unnamed Samaritan woman.

Jesus is not disturbed by this interruption but sees it as an opportunity to invite this woman to a conversion of heart. And in doing so, he teaches us a lesson on prayer. Jesus speaks first. He initiates the conversation.

Even though she was coming to the well for water herself, he addresses her, saying, "Give me a drink."

The Samaritan woman shows surprise: "How can you, a Jew, ask me, a Samaritan woman for a drink?" As a woman, she expected to be ignored. Furthermore, as a Samaritan woman, she could not believe that a Jew would even talk to her. Such an encounter never happened. But from Jesus she received respect and understanding.

Jesus then said to her: "If you knew the gift of God and who is saying to you, 'Give me a drink,' you would have asked him and he would have given you living water." For St. John, in whose gospel this dialogue is found, the "gift of God" is the Holy Spirit. Jesus was saying that if she knew that he could give her the Holy Spirit, that the Holy Spirit would be gushing in her like a fountain of water. And that is his gift to her and to each of us.

The Catechism teaches: "Every time we begin to pray to Jesus it is the Holy Spirit who draws us on the way of prayer" (CCC 2670). "The Holy Spirit, whose anointing permeates our whole being, is the interior Master of Christian prayer. He is the artisan of the living tradition of prayer" (CCC 2672). In this sense, prayer is the gift of God's Holy Spirit.

Pointing to the well, Jesus says: "Everyone who drinks this water will be thirsty again but whoever drinks the water I shall give will never thirst; the water I shall give will become in him a spring of water welling up to eternal life." St. Hippolytus (in a sermon on the Epiphany) describes this water as "the water of the Spirit. . . . It is the water of Christ's baptism; it is our life." Yes, by Baptism, we become temples of the Holy

Spirit. The Holy Spirit is like a fountain of water welling up within us. The woman then said to Jesus: "Sir give me this water, so that I may not be thirsty or have to keep coming here to draw water."

How does this particular passage, this encounter between Jesus and the Samaritan woman, deepen our understanding of prayer? The Catechism gives us a clear answer:

> "If you knew the gift of God!" The wonder of prayer is revealed beside the well where we come seeking water: there, Christ comes to meet every human being. It is he who first seeks us and asks us for a drink. Jesus thirsts; his asking arises from the depths of God's desire for us. Whether we realize it or not, prayer is the encounter of God's thirst with ours. God thirsts that we may thirst for him. (CCC 2560)

Yes, prayer is God's gift to us. It is the power of his Holy Spirit gushing like a fountain within us. And he is always taking the initiative. From the Common Preface IV at Mass, we pray: "Father . . . You have no need of our praise, yet our thanksgiving is itself your gift." In effect, our desire to pray is his gift.

The Initiative of God

So often, we view prayer primarily as our initiative. We think we need to master one of the thousand how-to books on prayer before we can even begin. This erroneous belief may even impede us from prayer.

Prayer often intimidates us. We view it as complicated or confusing, difficult, perplexing, and mysterious.

What the Catechism teaches from the very beginning is quite the opposite. At its basis, prayer is God's initiative in our lives. He comes to us. He comes to everyone as he came to the least likely person, a Samaritan woman. We are no different. That should give us encouragement as we seek to pray in our lives. That should give us a renewed sense of confidence.

Hopefully, that thought is reassuring. When you begin to pray, always remember Jesus—tired from his journey—taking the initiative at the well with a foreign woman, a Samaritan woman. "God thirsts that we may thirst for him" (*CCC* 2560). That is prayer. Pope Benedict teaches, moreover: "Each one of us can identify ourselves with the Samaritan woman: Jesus awaits us . . . to speak to our hearts, to my heart. Let us pause a moment in silence, in our room, or in a church, or in a place apart. Let us listen to the voice that says: 'If you knew the gift of God'" (Angelus, March 27, 2011). Listening is prayer.

Each of us, without exception, thirsts for God, for a God who is beyond us and yet near to us. As we travel on our life journeys, often tired from the challenges we face, it is in that very thirst, that desire for an oasis where our thirst can be quenched, that we find him. It is our deepest longing. The surge toward heaven in our hearts is God's action, the action of his Holy Spirit within us. When we yield to God, to God's actions within us, it is then that we pray. The gift of prayer is God's most generous and wonderful gift to us.

I conclude this chapter with the beautiful words of St. John Chrysostom. He writes:

Prayer stands before God as an honored ambassador. It gives joy to the spirit, peace to the heart. I speak of prayer, not words. It is the longing for God, love too deep for words, a gift not given by man but by God's grace. The apostle Paul says: *We do not know how we are to pray but the Spirit himself pleads for us with inexpressible longings.*

A Witness to Prayer

It has been said that until you are convinced that prayer is the best use of your time, you will not find time for prayer. Therein lies the challenge for most of us—finding time. Not surprisingly, many discover the real need to find that time and honor its sacredness only when they learn the sad and painful consequences of not praying. It is often only when one finds oneself adrift on the sea of life in search of a renewed sense of purpose and meaning that a person begins to recognize anew the need for and impact of regular prayer in one's life. As the timeless words of the ever ancient and ever new Psalm 90 so aptly notes: "Teach us, O Lord, the shortness of our days that we might live them with wisdom of heart." It is genuine wisdom of heart that informs our mind of the need to find time to pray. And it will always be the abundant graces of the loving "Hound of Heaven" that will help each of us to repeatedly succeed in finding that time in our lives regardless of how busy we may think ourselves to be.

—Msgr. Joseph G. Quinn

Reflect

1. Is there a particular time of day that you try to set aside for prayer? How is this practice helpful for you?

2. How does thinking of prayer as God's gift to you rather than something you do for God affect your approach to prayer?

Pray

A Morning Offering

Into your hands, O God, we commend ourselves this day, and all those who are dear to us. Let the gift of your wonderful presence be with us even to the end of the day. Grant that we never lose sight of you all the day long, but rather praise and beseech you that our thanks may come to you again at its close. Amen.

—Gelasian Sacramentary

two

Old Testament Models of Prayer

Even though the title of the last section of the Catechism is "Christian Prayer," the Catechism includes significant passages on prayer in the Old Testament. The Old Testament is, after all, a powerhouse of prayer, and there is much to learn about prayer from understanding how our ancestors in the faith prayed. The Old Testament is, moreover, God's living and revealed Word. As the Catechism emphasizes, "the revelation of prayer comes between the fall and the restoration of man" (*CCC* 2568).

Our personal prayer lives are enriched by God's holy and spoken words from the Old Testament. Prayer unfolds in all of salvation history, "for it is the relationship with God in historical events" (*CCC* 2568). So it was with Abraham, Jacob, Moses, David, Elijah, and all of our ancestors in faith. They were very familiar with God in prayer. They lived and breathed in the presence of God.

God's Promise and
the Prayer of Faith—Abraham and Jacob

What do we learn about prayer from the Old Testament? Since prayer is bound up with human history, we certainly acknowledge at the outset that there is much human history in the relationship between God and us that is told in the Old Testament beginning with the creation stories of Genesis and ending with the Book of Malachi. "In the indefectible covenant with every living creature, God has always called people to prayer. But it is above all beginning with our father Abraham that prayer is revealed in the Old Testament" (*CCC* 2569).

In Genesis, after God promises to the great patriarch Abraham that he will make of him a great nation and he will bless him, we learn that Abraham, our father in faith, went forth "as the Lord directed him" (Gn 12:4).

> Abraham's heart is entirely submissive to the Word and so he obeys. Such attentiveness of the heart, whose decisions are made according to God's will, is essential to prayer. . . . Abraham's prayer is expressed first by deeds: a man of silence, he constructs an altar to the Lord at each stage of his journey. (*CCC* 2570)

But it was not always easy for Abraham. Nor is it easy for us. Gradually, there is a veiled complaint from Abraham to God. "Abram said, 'O Lord God, what good will your gifts be, if I keep on being childless. . . .

See, you have given me no offspring, and so one of my servants will be my heir.' Then the word of the Lord came to him: 'No, that one shall not be your heir; your own issue shall be your heir'" (Gn 15:2–5). With that reassurance, Abraham put his faith in the Lord.

That exchange teaches us, however, of "one aspect of the drama of prayer [which] appears from the beginning: the test of faith in the fidelity of God" (CCC 2570). It is no different with us. Sometimes we wonder whether God is even listening to our prayers, fulfilling his promises to us. In time, we begin to appreciate that such wondering can lead to a prayerful trust in him who can, indeed, work wonders in our lives and in the lives of those we love.

There is another side to the prayer of Abraham—his compassionate willingness to intercede with bold confidence on behalf of the inhabitants of two cities, Sodom and Gomorrah. We learn in Genesis 18 of his prayerful intercession seeking to convince God not to carry out an act of justice and halt the evil by destroying these two cities. He had confidence in the mercy of God to try and intercede on behalf of the innocent people living in Sodom and Gomorrah. He asked God to spare the cities if enough innocent people were found there.

Commenting on this passage, Pope Benedict states: "Through Abraham's intercession, Sodom can be saved if there are even only ten innocent people in it." He concludes, "This is the power of prayer. For through intercession, the prayer to God for the salvation of others, the desire for salvation which God nourishes for sinful man is demonstrated and expressed." But he states further that "evil, in fact, cannot be accepted, it must be identified and destroyed through punishment:

The destruction of Sodom had exactly this function" (Audience, May 18, 2011). This destruction happened despite the prayerful intercession of the great patriarch Abraham.

At a later time, Abraham, who had awaited the birth of a child for so long, was challenged by God to sacrifice his son Isaac. God put him to the test telling him to "take your son Isaac, your only one, whom you love, and go to the land of Moriah. There you shall offer him up as a holocaust on a height that I will point out to you" (Gn 22:1–2). But as he was preparing to carry out this order, the Lord's messenger told him not to carry it out and Isaac was spared. "And so the father of believers is conformed to the likeness of the Father who will not spare his own Son but will deliver him up for us all. Prayer restores man to God's likeness and enables him to share in the power of God's love that saves the multitude" (CCC 2572).

The story of the Patriarch Jacob in Genesis 32:24–30 presents yet another dimension of prayer. It is the story of Jacob's wrestling all night with a mysterious figure who refuses to reveal his name. The man blesses him at dawn when Jacob finally comes to realize that he was in effect wrestling with God. This is a story of the perseverance in prayer. How can we not think of the persistent widow in Luke 18:1–8? Or the prayer of Jesus at Gethsemane and his struggle between his will and the will of his Father? "From this account [of Jacob], the spiritual tradition of the Church has retained the symbol of prayer as a battle of faith and as a triumph of perseverance" (CCC 2573). Benedict XVI describes this text in the following way: "The Bible text speaks to us about a long night of seeking God, of the struggle to learn his name and see his face; it is the night of prayer that, with tenacity and perseverance, asks God for a blessing and a new name, a new reality that is the fruit of conversion and forgiveness" (Audience, May 25, 2011). With perseverance in prayer, we too can see the face of God and achieve a sense of interior renewal in the Lord.

God's Initiative and Moses's Response

Moses was a man of prayer, a bearer of the commandments, and leader to the Promised Land. In Exodus 3 Moses experiences the initiative of God in his life, not unlike the experience of the Samaritan woman. As you read the following passage, place yourself at Mount Horeb with Moses and God. From the midst of the burning bush, God calls Moses:

> "Moses! Moses!" He answered, "Here I am." God said, "Come no nearer! Remove the sandals from your feet, for the place where you stand is holy ground. I am the God of your father," he continued, "the God of Abraham, the God of Isaac, the God of Jacob." Moses hid his face, for he was afraid to look at God. But the Lord said, "I have witnessed the affliction of my people in Egypt and have heard their cry of complaint against their slave drivers, so I know well what they are suffering. Therefore I have come down to rescue them from the hands of the Egyptians

> and lead them out of that land into a
> good and spacious land, a land flow-
> ing with milk and honey, the country of
> the Canaanites, Hittites, Amorites, Per-
> izzites, Hivites and Jebusites. . . . Come,
> now! I will send you to Pharaoh to lead
> my people, the Israelites, out of Egypt."
> (Ex 3:4–8, 10)

This event in the life of Moses remains "one of the primordial images of prayer in the spiritual tradition of Jews and Christians alike. When 'the God of Abraham, of Isaac, and Jacob' calls Moses to be his servant, it is because he is the living God who wants men to live. . . . He calls Moses to be his messenger, an associate in his compassion, his work of salvation" (*CCC* 2575).

Moses responds to the call of God by saying simply, "Here I am." Even though prayer is fundamentally the initiative of our persistent, loving God (in the same way that Jesus took the initiative with the Samaritan woman), it requires a response from us. God calls, we listen and respond, "Here I am." This is the model we see time and again in the scriptures.

How often do we come onto holy ground? How often do we say to the Lord, "Here I am"? Before we can say that, before we can approach him with trepidation and fear, we need first to find time to be with him each and every day, each and every moment of the day. It is easy to ignore God, to live as if he does not exist. Yet for those who are alert, there are repeated signs of his presence. It may not be a burning bush that gets our attention. The sign will assuredly be subtler. It might be the witness of a friend, a spouse, a movement of the Holy Spirit within us. Perhaps it will take place at work, as it did for Moses, who was leading his flock across the desert when he saw the bush on fire but not consumed. The Lord continues to call us, to thirst after us. His thirst for us makes us thirsty for him. In the words of St. Augustine, "Our hearts are restless until they rest in you."

In Genesis, the first book of the Bible, we hear of Noah who "found favor with the Lord . . . for he walked with God" (Gn 6:8, 10). We can walk with God too. That is what prayer is. It is a call to walk with God.

Moses's Prayer of Intercession

Our focus now shifts from Moses's early encounter with God in the burning bush to his later encounters with God on Mount Sinai as he led the Israelites through the desert. Mount Sinai is not only the place where Moses received the Ten Commandments; it is also the place where he spoke to God and God spoke to him. "Moses converses with God often and at length, climbing the mountain to hear and entreat him and coming down to the people to repeat the words of his God for their guidance" (*CCC* 2576). What does this experience of Moses tell us about prayer? The Catechism teaches, "the prayer of Moses becomes the most striking example of intercessory prayer" (*CCC* 2574).

Consider the image of the golden calf. The Israelites began to wonder why Moses did not come down from the mountain, and in exasperation, they made a golden calf and began to worship it.

> With that, the Lord said to Moses, "Go down at once to your people, whom

you brought out of the land of Egypt,
for they have become depraved. They
have soon turned aside from the way I
pointed out to them, making for themselves a molten calf and worshiping it,
sacrificing to it and crying out, 'This is
your God, O Israel, who brought you
out of the land of Egypt!' I see how stiff-
necked this people is," continued the
Lord to Moses. (Ex 32:7–9)

Pope Benedict XVI, reflecting on the construction of
the molten calf, broadens the implications to our own
day: "This is the constant temptation on the journey
of faith: to avoid the divine mystery by constructing a
comprehensible god who corresponds with one's own
plans, one's own projects" (Audience, June 1, 2011).

God threatened to consume his people because
of their idolatry. In response, we hear the courageous
words of Moses, who implored the Lord:

"Why, O Lord, should your wrath blaze
up against your own people, whom you
brought out of the land of Egypt with
such great power and with so strong a
hand? Why should the Egyptians say,
'With evil intent he brought them out,
that he might kill them in the mountains
and exterminate them from the face of
the earth'? Let your blazing wrath die
down; relent in punishing your people. Remember your servants Abraham,
Isaac and Israel, and how you swore to
them by your own self, saying, 'I will

make your descendants as numerous
as the stars in the sky; and all this land
that I promised, I will give your descendants as their perpetual heritage,'" So
the Lord relented in the punishment he
had threatened to inflict on his people.

Moses then turned and came down
the mountain with the two tablets of
the commandments in his hands, tablets that were written on both sides,
front and back; tablets that were made
by God, having inscriptions on them
that were engraved by God himself. (Ex
32:11–16)

That was not sufficient. The story continues. The
Israelites continued in their apostasy.

On the next day Moses said to the people, "You have committed a grave sin.
I will go up to the Lord, then; perhaps
I may be able to make atonement for
your sin." So Moses went back to the
Lord and said, "Ah, this people has
indeed committed a grave sin in making a god of gold for themselves! If you
would only forgive their sin! If you will
not, then strike me out of the book that
you have written." The Lord answered,
"Him only who has sinned against me
will I strike out of my book. Now, go
and lead the people whither I have told
you. My angel will go before you. When
it is time for me to punish, I will punish

them for their sin." Thus the Lord smote
the people for having had Aaron make
the calf for them. (Ex 32:30–35)

In this intercessory dialogue between God and
Moses, Moses "learns how to pray: he balks, makes
excuses, above all questions: and it is in response to
his question that the Lord confides his ineffable name,
which will be revealed through his mighty deeds"
(*CCC* 2575).

From this intimacy with the faithful
God, slow to anger and abounding in
steadfast love, Moses drew strength
and determination for his intercession.
He does not pray for himself but for
the people whom God made his own.
. . . But it is chiefly after their apostasy that Moses "stands in the breach"
before God in order to save the people.
The arguments of his prayer—for intercession is also a mysterious battle—will
inspire the boldness of the great intercessors among the Jewish people and in
the Church. (*CCC* 2577)

In fact, as the *United States Catholic Catechism for
Adults* teaches: "Moses dramatized the value of intercessory prayer as he vigorously begged God for mercy
and guidance for the people making their journey to
the Promised Land" (*USCCA* 464).

It should inspire us. How are others to know the
Lord Jesus if we do not pray for them, and pray for
them by name, especially when they are in trouble or
when they have turned from the Lord? Moses is that

great example of intercessory prayer. He is also our model. He went to the proverbial "mat" for his people. It should be no different with us.

The Prayer of the People of God—Samuel, David, and Solomon

The prayer of the People of God flourished, moreover, in the shadow of God's dwelling place. That took place first in the shadow of God's presence in the Ark of the Covenant and later in the Temple.

Of special note is Samuel, the last of the judges and a prophet, who heard the voice of the Lord while asleep. His well-known response is often the mantra of people at prayer to this day: "Speak, Lord, for your servant is listening" (1 Sm 3:9). "Listening," after all, to the voice of the Lord rests at the heart of genuine prayer. Samuel will later know the cost or consequences of prayerful intercession for he says, "As for me, far be it from me to sin against the Lord by ceasing to pray for you and to teach you the good and right way" (1 Sm 13:23).

It was Samuel who anointed David as king. King David was a model of prayer for his people: "His prayer, the prayer of God's Anointed, is a faithful adherence to the divine promise and expresses a loving and joyful trust in God, the only King and Lord" (CCC 2579). He was the shepherd who prayed for his people and in their name. His was a prayer of submission, praise, and repentance. In the psalms, prayers inspired by the Holy Spirit, David becomes the first prophet of Jewish and Christian prayer, a prayer Christ would later fulfill and reveal its meaning in his very person.

The prayer of King David's son, Solomon, at the dedication of the Temple is worth pondering. As he outstretched his arms at the dedication of the Temple, where the Ark of the Covenant was lodged, the Ark that held the tablets of the commandments and symbolized the living presence of God among his people, he prayed:

> Look kindly on the prayer and petition of your servant, O Lord, my God, and listen to the cry of supplication which I, your servant, utter before you this day. May your eyes watch night and day over this temple, the place where you have decreed you shall be honored; may you heed the prayer which I, your servant, offer in this place. Listen to the petitions of your servant and of your people Israel that they offer in this place. Listen from your heavenly dwelling and grant pardon. (1 Kgs 8:28–30)

The Catechism teaches: "For the People of God, the Temple was to be the place of their education in prayer: pilgrimages, feasts and sacrifices, the evening offering, the incense, and the bread of the Presence ('shewbread')—all these signs of the holiness and glory of God Most High and Most Near were appeals to and ways of prayer" (CCC 2581).

As Catholics, we find that the proper place for liturgical prayer is the Church, the successor to the Temple, the house of God. We are reminded that "it is also the privileged place for adoration of the real presence of Christ in the Blessed Sacrament" (CCC 2691).

The holiness that surrounded the Ark of the Covenant in the Temple surrounds the tabernacle where the real presence of God is reserved in the Blessed Sacrament.

> "The Catholic Church has always offered and still offers to the sacrament of the Eucharist the cult of adoration, not only during Mass, but also outside of it, reserving the consecrated hosts with the utmost care, exposing them to the solemn veneration of the faithful, and carrying them in procession. . . ." In his Eucharistic presence he remains mysteriously in our midst as the one who loved us and gave himself up for us. (CCC 1378, 1380)

The Prayer of the Assembly—The Psalms

Finally, we turn to the psalms. The Catechism calls the psalms "the masterwork of prayer in the Old Testament" (CCC 2585). The psalms have variously been referred to as the "great prayer book" of sacred scripture and also a "school of prayer."

> They embraced every age of history, while being rooted in each moment of time. They were sung at the Temple, in local synagogues, in family settings, on pilgrimages, and in the solitude of personal prayer. They formed the basis of the prayer of Jesus and, as such, can be

used to draw us into his prayer as well.
(*USCCA* 465)

These prayers of praise, which appeared from
the time of David to the coming of the Messiah, were
gradually collected into five books called the Psalter—150 psalms. Pope Benedict XVI, speaking about
the psalms, states: "In this book, the whole human
experience with its multiple facets finds expression,
along with the entire range of emotions that accom-
pany man's existence" (Audience, June 22, 2011). In
his apostolic constitution *Divino Afflatu*, Pope St. Pius
X writes, moreover: "The collection of psalms found in
Scripture, composed as it was under divine inspiration,
has, from the very beginnings of the Church, shown a
wonderful power of fostering devotion among Christians as they offer *to God a continuous sacrifice of praise,
the harvest of lips blessing his name.*"

The psalms are not composed in a narrative story.
Instead, the texts of prayer have as their primary function the ability of becoming the prayer of the one who
uses these texts to address God. They are primarily
prayers of praise and petition and inseparably personal and communal. Benedict XVI teaches further that:
"Since they are the word of God, anyone who prays the
psalms speaks to God using the very words that God
has given to us, addresses him with the words that he
himself has given us" (Audience, June 22, 2011).

Those who are ordained have promised to pray the
Liturgy of the Hours (or the Divine Office) each day
for God's holy people. It is in effect the prayer of the
Church, with Christ and to Christ. The Liturgy of the
Hours is meant as well to sanctify each hour of the day.
A significant part of the Liturgy of the Hours is the

psalms that members of the clergy and religious pray. Many lay people have also adopted this wonderful daily practice. The psalms are a great treasury for us from the Hebrew Scriptures. At each and every Mass, the responsorial psalm is from the Psalter. They have become an integral part of our liturgy.

Praying the psalms, whether personally or communally, can be challenging. It is helpful to remember "the Psalms are a mirror of God's marvelous deeds in the history of his people, as well as reflections of the human experiences of the Psalmist" (*CCC* 2588). Professor Lawrence S. Cunningham of the University of Notre Dame reflects on our entry into the prayerful use of the psalms:

> To enter the world of the psalms is, in short, to enter the world of the other, an other who has had profound experiences of God with which I can frequently resonate. The psalmist sometimes depicts God as distant, majestic, worthy of adoration from afar. That same God, in the same psalm, can quickly then show himself as close, intimate and caring. It is as if a camera is moving from a long, panoramic shot to a close-up. In Psalm 9, for example, God is depicted as "enthroned forever," but that cosmic sense of God enthroned (over the cosmos, over the Ark of the Covenant in the Temple) quickly shifts in verse nine to the God who is "Lord of the oppressed." That shift from distant majesty to concerned immediacy recurs

continually within individual psalms.
Distance and intimacy are markers of
the deepest spirituality and full sensi-
bility of the psalmist.

Prayed by Christ and fulfilled in him, the psalms
are an essential and permanent element of the prayer
of the Church. They are also a great contribution of the
Old Testament to our prayer lives.

A Witness to Prayer

The image that I can best use to describe what
prayer means to me is that prayer is like a school.
In this school I learn about God who created me
and all of the people I encounter each day, the
Church in which we share our faith, and the world
in which we live. I come to know more about God
by listening to his word in scripture, especially in
the words and works of Jesus, and by paying close
attention to the words God speaks to my heart.

I also come to learn about myself in this school
of prayer. I learn how to relate to God, others, and
myself in loving ways. I learn about the things
that are stumbling blocks for me and learn how to
trust that God will guide me through them. Most
importantly in prayer I learn of the limitlessness
of God's love and grace, and I come before him
with humility and gratitude to give glory to his
name, to thank him for being a master teacher, and
to try as best as I can to return to God the love that
has been given to me.

—Sr. Rachel Terry

Reflect

1. Abraham experienced many tests of faith, yet always remained faithful. How do you pray when it may seem that God is not listening?

2. What are the lessons we can learn from Abraham and Moses about the prayer of intercession?

3. What are some of the people, places, and things that draw your attention to God as the burning bush did for Moses?

Pray

Psalm 40

I waited, I waited for the Lord
and he stooped down to me;
he heard my cry.

He drew me from the deadly pit,
from the miry clay.
He set my feet upon a rock
and made my footsteps firm.

He put a new song into my mouth,
praise of our God.
Many shall see and fear
and shall trust in the Lord.

Happy the man who has placed
his trust in the Lord
and has not gone over to the rebels
who follow false gods.

How many, O Lord my God,
are the wonders and designs
that you have worked for us;
you have no equal.
Should I proclaim and speak of them,
they are more than I can tell!

You do not ask for sacrifice and offerings,
but an open ear.
You do not ask for holocaust and victim.
Instead, here am I.

In the scroll of the book it stands written
that I should do your will.
My God, I delight in your law
in the depth of my heart.

Your justice I have proclaimed
in the great assembly.
My lips I have not sealed;
you know it, O Lord.

I have not hidden your justice in my heart
but declared your faithful help.
I have not hidden your love and your truth
from the great assembly.

—The Grail Psalter

three

Jesus, the Master of Prayer

Jesus was a master craftsman, a master artist like Michelangelo or Giotto. Watching Jesus at prayer is like observing a master artist at work. Perhaps you have never thought of Jesus in this way before. His prayer is original and unique. It is a consistent part of his life and ministry.

In *Jesus Christ: Word of the Father, the Savior of the World*, prepared by the Theological-Historical Commission for the Great Jubilee of the Year 2000, we read:

> It is useful to rediscover Christian prayer today by contemplating the icon of Jesus in prayer. This is a fascinating side of Jesus' personality that has created an authentic, millennial tradition of Christian spirituality and holiness that is waiting to be rediscovered and to be made the most of. Jesus' originality in this field has been grasped even by non-Christians, who see in him not only a pious Jew, but above all an unsurpassable master of spiritual life and intimacy with God.

The Catechism describes beautifully the icon of Jesus at prayer. We see that Jesus prays, teaches us how to pray, and hears our prayers. That Jesus prayed is perhaps one of the best-documented aspects of the historical Jesus. He was a master at prayer. He was often absorbed in prayer.

Jesus Prays

All of Jesus' daily life—morning, midday and night—was rooted in prayer. He often retreated to the desert or a mountain to pray (Mk 1:35; Lk 5:16; Mt. 4:l). He rose early to pray (Mk 1:35) and often spent the entire night at prayer as he did before choosing the twelve apostles (Lk 6:12).

Like us, Jesus had to learn to pray. He learned from his mother Mary. He learned in the synagogue and at the Temple. He prayed the psalms, the same ones that we pray today. But there was something unique and different about Jesus' prayer from the very beginning. Already at age twelve, he knew instinctively that his prayer sprung from "an otherwise secret source" (CCC 2599). When he was found in the Temple, he said: "I must be in my Father's house" (Lk 2:49). Even at a young age, he knew God like no one else did.

The prayer of Jesus is unique. It is filial prayer. It expresses that consistent and life-giving relationship that as Son of God he had with his Father. "Jesus' filial prayer is the perfect model of prayer in the New Testament. Often done in solitude and in secret, the prayer of Jesus involves a loving adherence to the will of the Father even to the Cross and an absolute confidence in being heard" (CCC 2620).

There are many biblical citations of Jesus at prayer in all the gospels. In particular, biblical scholars have referred to Luke as the "gospel of prayer" because in it we so often find Jesus at prayer. It is interesting to underscore that throughout the entire gospel, Jesus prays before every decisive moment of his life and mission. He often prays in solitude and at night.

In Luke's gospel, Jesus was at prayer as he was being baptized, and he was at prayer at the very moment that God the Father revealed his identity and his mission by saying: "You are my beloved Son; with you I am well pleased" (Lk 3:21–22). Before the calling of the apostles, "He departed to the mountain to pray, and he spent the night in prayer to God" (Lk 6:12). In all the accounts of the multiplication of the loaves and fishes, we see Jesus "looking up to heaven [and saying] the blessing" (Lk 9:16). In the Transfiguration of the Lord, Jesus took "Peter, John, and James and went up the mountain to pray. While he was praying his faced changed in appearance and his clothing became dazzling white" (Lk 9:28–29). His very identity as Son of God was thus revealed during prayer for all to see. When he posed the question, "Who do the crowds say that I am?" and Peter recognized him as the Messiah, "Jesus was praying in solitude" (Lk 9:18). *Before* he taught the Lord's Prayer, "He was praying in a certain place, and when he had finished, one of his disciples said to him, 'Lord, teach us to pray'" (Lk 11:1).

The Theological-Historical Commission also reminded us:

> Prayer enables the incarnate Word to remain with the Father, to be turned continually toward Him and wholly gathered in His bosom. Although he came to dwell in our midst, Jesus never

distanced himself from communion
with the Father in prayer. Inasmuch as
his prayer was a continual act of filial
obedience—"not my will, but thine be
done" (Lk 22:42)—it is also the basis
of His mission. . . . By his prayer, Jesus
shows that He did not merely preach
and practice an ethical or social gospel, but also lived an intense spiritual
life. Indeed, this rooting in the Father's
heart was the source of His apostolic
dynamism. This is one of the aspects
that Christian pastoral ministry most
has to recover today.

Thanksgiving is a very important theme in Jesus'
prayer to his Father. In Matthew 11:25, Jesus says from
the depth of his heart: "I give praise to you, Father."
In John 11:41–42, *before* the raising of Lazarus, Jesus
gives thanks to the Father. "Father, I thank you for
hearing me. I know that you always hear me." And
then he raised Lazarus from the dead. So, too, each of
us should give thanks to God, as Jesus did, even before
our petition is made or the gift given. "The Giver is
more precious than the gift; he is the 'treasure'; in him
abides his Son's heart; the gift is given as well" (*CCC*
2604).

Jesus Teaches Us to Pray

Both Matthew (6:9–13) and Luke (11:1–4) include
the Lord's Prayer. (We will look more closely at this
prayer in chapter 9.) Jesus not only prayed, he *explicitly*

taught his disciples how to pray. Citing Tertullian, the Catechism states: "The Lord's Prayer is truly the summary of the whole Gospel" (*CCC* 2761). Jesus taught them to pray to the Father using the word *abba* "which in the language of his day was used by children to speak to their fathers" (*USCCA* 466). He taught them to make holy his name, to pray that his kingdom will come and that his will be done. He taught them to ask for enough bread for this day, forgiveness of trespasses, protection from temptation and the evil one. What a wonderful prayer of hope—all that there is to pray for is included! What a master of prayer Jesus is!

I was struck that Jesus not only taught prayer but he put that prayer into action on two specific occasions. Near the end of his life at the Last Supper, John records that Jesus raised his eyes in prayer and—speaking of his followers—said to the Father: "I do not ask that you take them out of this world but that you keep them from the evil one" (Jn 17:15). As he had taught his disciples to do, Jesus prayed on the cross for forgiveness saying, "Father, forgive them, they know not what they do" (Lk 23:34). (Chapters 6 and 7 will examine Jesus' prayer at the Last Supper, at Gethsemane, and from the cross in great depth.)

Note well that Jesus always addresses his prayer to the Father at the Last Supper, from the Cross, in the Lord's Prayer, and in all his prayers. Obedience to the Father's will is at the center of his prayer. It is what makes his kind of prayer novel and unique. Even at Gethsemane, where Jesus' human will is tragically tested by suffering and pain, he confirms his oblation to the will of his Father. In so doing, he is also teaching *us* how to pray.

Jesus wants us to share in his filial relationship with his Father. He wants us to become sons and daughters of God (which we have become at Baptism), and he wants us to see the Father as he sees him. By watching Christ at prayer, in the power of the Holy Spirit, we can see the Father. As the master of prayer, he teaches us to trust his Father. "Like a wise teacher he takes hold of us where we are and leads us progressively towards the Father" (*CCC* 2607).

Watch carefully! Keep your eyes and hearts fixed on Jesus. Watch his prayer to the Father. He is the master! But what do we look for? There are five dimensions of prayer given us by Jesus.

Conversion of Heart. First, Jesus insists on a conversion of heart when we pray. He requires "reconciliation with one's brother before presenting an offering on the altar, love of enemies, and prayer for persecutors, prayer to the Father in secret, not heaping up empty phrases, prayerful forgiveness from the depths of the heart, purity of heart, and seeking the kingdom before all else. This filial conversion is entirely directed to the Father" (*CCC* 2608).

Prayer in Faith. Second, after we have made the commitment to open our hearts in this way—and it is a daily and lifetime challenge—"the heart learns to pray in faith" (*CCC* 2609). We firmly cling to the Father even when we feel our prayers are not being answered. Faith, after all, is filial adherence to God beyond what we feel and understand. Seek and knock for he himself is the door and way.

Boldness. Third, Jesus teaches us filial boldness, the opposite of timidity. "Whatever you ask in prayer, believe that you receive it, and you will" (*CCC* 2610).

Vigilance. Fourth, Jesus calls his disciples to a certain watchfulness and vigilance in being attentive to him in prayer.

In Jesus' Name. And finally, the fifth point, Jesus invites his disciples, and each of us, to present our petitions to the Father "in his name." This is a new dimension to prayer—to pray in his name.

Jesus Hears Our Prayers

Jesus Christ also answers prayers addressed to him. His entire healing ministry is ample evidence of that. This is particularly so when the prayer is offered in faith. "Your faith has made you well; go in peace" (*CCC* 2616). The healing of the paralytic underscores as well the faith of the four men who brought the paralytic to Jesus for healing. "When Jesus saw *their* faith, he said to the paralytic, 'Child, your sins are forgiven'" (Mk 2:5). Thereafter, he was physically healed. Another example of a person's faith and a subsequent healing is the woman afflicted with hemorrhages. In an act of faith, she touched the cloak of Jesus and "at once power had gone out from him" (Mk 5:30). And Jesus said to her: "Daughter, your faith has saved you. Go in peace and be cured of your affliction" (Mk 5:34). The faith of the leper in Mark's gospel is another example of Jesus' healing response to a person of faith. The leper begged Jesus and said to him: "If you wish, you can make me clean" (Mk 1:40). Jesus touched him and said to him: "I do will it. Be made clean" (Mk 1:41). And the leprosy left him immediately.

The Prayer of the Virgin Mary

At the end of its chapter on Jesus at prayer, the Catechism appropriately includes a section on the prayer of Mary, the Mother of Jesus and the Mother of the Church. Specifically, it treats her *fiat* (her yes) at the Annunciation, her intercessory prayer at the wedding feast of Cana, and her great prayer of praise, the Magnificat.

In response to the angel Gabriel at the Annunciation, "She whom the Almighty made 'full of grace' responds by offering her whole being: 'Behold I am the handmaid of the Lord; let it be [done] to me according to your word.' 'Fiat': this is Christian prayer: to be wholly God's, because he is wholly ours" (CCC 2617). It is expressed in the many circumstances each day when we humbly seek to discern the will of God for us. In her fiat, Mary became a vessel and instrument of God's grace in a totally unique and powerful way, a profound model for each of us in a different way.

At the wedding feast of Cana, Mary models her prayer, a prayer of intercession and maternal concern for the needs of the bridal couple. Mary is a powerful intercessor. How can we ever forget those powerful words of Mary—"Do whatever he tells you" (Jn 2:5)? Nor how can we ever forget the words of the Memorare: "Remember O most gracious Virgin Mary that never was it known that anyone who fled to thy protection, implored thy help, or sought thy intercession was left unaided." Mary is a powerful intercessor.

Finally in her Magnificat, Mary unites the voices of many before and after her, "My soul proclaims the greatness of the Lord." Her canticle was one of the poor whose only hope lay in the fulfillment of the promises made "to Abraham and to his descendants forever" (Lk 1:46–55).

"'*Magnificat anima mea Dominum*,' she says on the occasion of that visit, 'My soul magnifies the Lord' (Lk 1:46). In these words she expresses her whole program of life: not setting herself at the centre, but leaving space for God, who is encountered both in prayer and in service of neighbor—only then does goodness enter the world" (*DCE* 41). A sense of gratitude was Mary's abiding disposition in her relationship with her Creator and Lord. So should it be in our prayer. Gratitude is a distinctive characteristic of genuine Christian prayer. This gratitude is expressed as we seek, like Mary, to leave a space for God.

The Challenge of Regular Prayer

Both Jesus and Mary gave themselves totally to God. They never gave up on prayer. They lived the will of God in their everyday lives. Jesus and Mary were entirely preoccupied with God and were intent on following his will no matter what the price and where it would lead.

Jesus, master and artisan of prayer, teaches us to pray. His mother models for us her abiding trust, concern, and gratitude, which is characteristic of all that Jesus taught and practiced himself. Not one of us should ever give up on prayer. Prayer was so central to the life of Jesus. We thus pray continually that our prayer might nourish and sustain us also.

Jesus thus prayed constantly and we are asked to do the same. After the example of Jesus, prayer is a heart-to-heart conversation with God. *Cor ad cor loqui-tur,* St. Augustine called it. Prayer is the Sacred Heart of Jesus touching and transforming our human hearts. Even our desire to pray is an act of prayer, for ultimately we pray only because of the Holy Spirit who prays within us. The Holy Spirit, after all, is the living breath of prayer.

For most of us, it is a challenge to make time to pray each day, to give God quality time and not simply junk time. It is so often hard to begin. Why not designate ten to fifteen minutes each day at a specific time and specific place? Perhaps choose the morning and evening as Jesus did—wonderful anchors of the day. It is a good practice to examine from time to time our prayer life. For example, do we pray the rosary? Do we read scripture regularly? Do we simply sit still long enough each day to recall God's presence in our lives and to praise and thank and love him? Jesus did.

What about public prayer? What about the Sacrament of Penance? Is Penance an anchor in your spiritual life? Wouldn't it be wonderful to receive that healing sacrament on a regular basis? What about the highest form of prayer—the Eucharist? Have you ever considered the Mass to be the highest form of prayer? Keep your eyes, then, fixed on Jesus, the master of prayer. "The drama of prayer is fully revealed to us in the Word who became flesh and dwells among us" (*CCC* 2598).

A Witness to Prayer

Prayer is the sacred place where I encounter
and receive from the God who pours his love

into my heart. It is an intimate place of solitude and quiet that refreshes my soul, guides the direction of my daily life, and where I am able to receive constantly the mercy, which enables me to continue along the path towards holiness. At times his gentle voice resounds in my heart in an indescribable beauty, and sometimes the voice remains in a longing silence, teaching me to seek him with an ever-deepening pure and undivided heart. Prayer allows the soul to plunge into the mysterious abyss of Trinitarian love without which the soul cannot survive.

—Msgr. Robert J. Panke

Reflect

1. Which of the many instances of Jesus at prayer speaks to you and calls you to deeper prayer?

2. Which of the five dimensions of Jesus' prayer are found in your prayer? Which may be lacking?

3. What difference does prayer make in your life? What may be lacking in your life that only prayer can supply?

Pray

Pray with Jesus as he prays for you.

Father, I revealed your name to those whom you

gave me out of the world. They belonged to you, and you gave them to me, and they have kept your word.

I pray for them. I do not pray for the world but for the ones you have given me, because they are yours, and everything of mine is yours and everything of yours is mine, and I have been glorified in them.

And now I will no longer be in the world, but they are in the world, while I am coming to you. Holy Father, keep them in your name that you have given me, so that they may be one just as we are.

When I was with them I protected them in your name that you gave me. . . .

But now I am coming to you. I speak this in the world so that they may share my joy completely.

I gave them your word, and the world hated them, because they do not belong to the world any more than I belong to the world. I do not ask that you take them out of the world but that you keep them from the evil one. They do not belong to the world any more than I belong to the world.

Consecrate them in the truth. Your word is truth. As you sent me into the world, so I sent them into the world. And I consecrate myself for them, so that they also may be consecrated in truth.

—John 17:6–19

four

Prayer in the Life of the Church

From the day of Pentecost and through the earliest days of the Church, the Acts of the Apostles tells us how the disciples gathered together to pray. Acts 1:14 shows us that while awaiting the coming of the Holy Spirit, the disciples "devoted themselves with one accord to prayer." We learn from Acts 2:42 that the first community of believers in Jerusalem devoted themselves to the teaching of the apostles, fellowship, breaking of the bread, and prayer. "The infant Church was born in prayer, lived in prayer, and thrived in prayer" (*USCCA* 467). It should be no different in our day.

In every age the Holy Spirit continues to teach the Church the ways of prayer. There is the prayer of adoration (our acknowledgment before God that we are his creatures); the prayer of petition (the evidence of our dependence on God); the prayer of intercession (requests of God on behalf of the needs of others); the prayer of thanksgiving (the posture of thanking God for all his blessings for us); and the prayer of praise (the continuing recognition that God is God).

God reveals the importance of prayer through sacred scripture. But he also continues to teach us about prayer through the life, worship, and doctrine of the Church. That is what we call Tradition. It has been handed down through the centuries and in the lives of those who have gone before us. It is passed on to us every day of our lives. One of the great benefits of being Catholic is our *long and living tradition* of prayer. We need not begin at square one and reinvent prayer. Prayer has been an integral part of our lives as followers of Jesus from the very beginning and it continues to be.

God also continues to reveal himself to us precisely when we are *at* prayer: when we celebrate the sacraments, listen to the Word proclaimed in the liturgy, or ponder a sacred text alone.

It is important to remember, "prayer cannot be reduced to the spontaneous outpouring of interior impulse" (*CCC* 2650). Prayer is a spiritual exercise, and no kind of exercise can take place without both the will to exercise *and* the knowledge of how to exercise. Like riding a bicycle, we need both the will to pray and the knowledge of how to pray.

But who teaches us to pray? In a word, it is the Holy Spirit. As St. Paul teaches: "The Spirit too comes to the aid of our weakness; for we do not know how to pray as we ought, but the Spirit itself intercedes with inexpressible groanings" (Rom 8:26). Blessed John Paul II used to say that the Holy Spirit is the "breath of prayer." And it is always good for us to come to know better this third person of the Blessed Trinity and how it is that the Holy Spirit reveals himself in our lives, particularly in our prayer lives. He is unpredictable. The Spirit moves where he will. As you look for the Holy Spirit, know that the Holy Spirit comes gently. The Spirit is never felt as a burden, for the Spirit is light. The Spirit comes with the tenderness of a true friend and protector to save, to heal, to teach, to counsel, to strengthen, and to console us. This is particularly so in our prayer.

The Wellsprings of Prayer

The Catechism repeatedly links the Holy Spirit to prayer. At the outset, it calls the Holy Spirit "the living water 'welling up to eternal life' in the heart that prays" (CCC 2652). The Catechism states also that "the Holy Spirit, whose anointing permeates our whole being, is the interior Master of Christian prayer. He is the artisan of the living tradition of prayer. . . . It is in the communion of the Holy Spirit that Christian prayer is prayer in the Church" (CCC 2672). The Catechism states in addition that "the Holy Spirit, who thus keeps the memory of Christ alive in his Church at prayer, also leads her toward the fullness of truth and inspires new formulations expressing the unfathomable mystery of Christ at work in his Church's life, sacraments, and mission" (CCC 2625). What a wonderful description of the Holy Spirit—"the breath of prayer," the interior master (and teacher) of prayer, the artisan of the living tradition of prayer, the living water welling up in the heart that prays. If the Holy Spirit is the living water, where then, you might ask, is the wellspring? The Catechism sets forth four such wellsprings "where Christ awaits us to enable us to drink of the Holy Spirit" (CCC 2652). And they are very practical.

The Word of God

God's holy Word is alive and active. It strikes to the heart like a two-edged sword. This happens precisely because of the Holy Spirit. Our challenge is to read his Word prayerfully each day (or if not, at least frequently). What a wonderful goal—to develop that prayerful dialogue between God and us, each and every day at a specific time in a specific place! We are challenged to receive God's Word, to listen to it from the heart, to reflect on it, to respond to it, and to relish it. His Word will change our lives.

I would suggest developing the habit of *lectio divina* ("divine reading"), which means reading sacred scripture in a reflective and meditative way. Archbishop Thomas Collins writes: "In lectio divina we seek not to master or to grasp the sacred text, but rather, prayerfully and silently, to come into the presence of God through it." In the post-synodal apostolic exhortation, *Verbum Domini*, Pope Benedict XVI sets forth the four basic steps to this encounter with Christ through sacred scripture in lectio divina. The steps include the reading of the text ("lectio"). Here we seek to listen to what the biblical text says in itself. Next comes meditation ("meditatio") where we ask what the biblical text says to each of us. This is followed by prayer ("oratio"). In prayer we speak to the Lord in response to his word. And finally, we conclude with contemplation ("contemplatio") and ponder the conversion of mind, heart and life that the Lord is asking of us (*VD* 87).

In her book, *The Beauty of Faith*, Jem Sullivan includes a helpful description by a twelfth-century contemplative monk named Guido II who wrote of lectio divina from its foundation in the monastic tradition:

> Reading seeks for the sweetness of a
> blessed life, meditation perceives it,
> prayer asks for it, contemplation tastes
> it. Reading, as it were, puts food whole
> into the mouth, meditation chews it and
> breaks it up, prayer extracts its flavor,
> contemplation is the sweetness itself
> that gladdens and refreshes.

Other spiritual writers have concluded: "Seek in reading and you will find in meditating; knock in mental prayer and it will be opened to you by contemplation" (*CCC* 2654).

The Liturgy of the Church

It is in the sacramental liturgy of the Church that Christ "proclaims, makes present, and communicates the mystery of salvation, which is continued in the heart that prays" in the power of the Holy Spirit (*CCC* 2655). This observation refers to all the sacraments, but I wish to emphasize the Eucharist. The mystery of our relationship with the living God is more deeply internalized and progressively assimilated by dwelling in prayer on the texts of the Liturgy—before, during, and after Mass. The Mass is, after all, the highest form of prayer, "the source" and "summit" of our lives as Christians (*SC* 10). We can never stop encouraging each other and those close and not so close to us to participate weekly at Sunday Mass and even at Mass during the week.

Vatican Council II, speaking of the Church praying and singing at Mass, emphasizes the presence of

Christ there, for Christ promised that: "Where two or three are gathered together in my name, there am I in the midst of them' (Mt 18:20)" (*SC* 7). Of all the prayers offered at Mass, Donald Cardinal Wuerl highlights the importance of the Eucharistic Prayer. He writes: "Through the Eucharistic Prayer, Jesus becomes really present among us, as he promised; and where Jesus abides, there is heaven."

The Theological Virtues

The theological virtues of faith, hope, and charity are also wellsprings of prayer. One enters prayer through the narrow gate of faith. We come to Mass, that highest form of prayer, because in faith we believe that a piece of bread will become the Body of Christ, the Son of God; and that a cup of wine will become his precious blood. This is a tremendous act of faith and a source of our prayer. Whenever we begin to pray, we draw on the gift of faith that was first given to us in Baptism.

The virtue of hope is likewise a gift. "The Holy Spirit, who instructs us to celebrate the liturgy in expectation of Christ's return, teaches us to pray in hope" (*CCC* 2657). The Our Father is the prayer of hope, par excellence. Following the Our Father at Mass, we pray: "Deliver us, Lord, we pray, from every evil, graciously grant peace in our days, that, by the help of your mercy, we may be always free from sin and safe from all distress, as we await the blessed hope and coming our Savior, Jesus Christ." Prayer must reflect our hope, and hope is a source of our prayer.

Love, too, is a source of prayer. And "the love of God has been poured into our hearts through the holy Spirit that has been given to us" (Rom 5:5). "Prayer, formed by the liturgical life, draws everything into the love by which we are loved in Christ and which enables us to respond to him by loving as he has loved us" (*CCC* 2658).

Today

Psalm 95 reminds us: "O that today you would hearken to his voice! Harden not your hearts" (Ps 95:7–8). The Holy Spirit is offered to us at all times—in the events of our everyday lives. This takes place in the *today* of our lives at home and when we are at work. Our challenge is to be aware of the presence of the living God and the movements of God in our lives, often in the little details of life at every moment of the day—to listen and to respond to him.

The Way of Prayer

Having spoken of the sources of prayer, we now consider the ways of prayer in our Church. "The Magisterium of the Church has the task of discerning the fidelity of these ways of praying to the tradition of apostolic faith; it is for pastors and catechists to explain their meaning, always in relation to Jesus Christ" (*CCC* 2663). We now look to the Trinity and our Blessed Lady.

Father, Son, and Holy Spirit

The Catechism teaches us that authentic Christian prayer is Trinitarian (i.e., it is addressed to the Father, Son, and Holy Spirit), and it is done in communion with the holy Mother of God.

At the heart of all prayer is Jesus Christ. We have access to the Father *only* if we pray "in the name" of Jesus (*CCC* 2664). He is what prayer is all about for those of us who are called Christians. I often reflect on what St. Patrick wore on his breastplate: "Christ before me, Christ behind me, Christ above me, Christ beneath me, Christ all around me, Christ in the mouth of friend and stranger." That is truly the meaning of prayer. Jesus is the one name that contains everything. The name *Jesus* means "Yahweh saves." "To pray 'Jesus' is to invoke Him and to call Him within us. His name is the only one that contains the presence it signifies" (*CCC* 2666).

At the same time, "And no one can say, 'Jesus is Lord,' except by the holy Spirit" (1 Cor 12:3). "Every time we begin to pray to Jesus it is the Holy Spirit who draws us on the way of prayer by his prevenient grace" (*CCC* 2670). In his book, *Crossing the Threshold of Hope*, Blessed John Paul II, when asked how, for whom, and for what do you pray, answered:

> You would have to ask the Holy Spirit! The pope prays as the Holy Spirit permits him to pray. I think he has to pray in a way in which, deepening the mystery revealed in Christ, he can better fulfill his ministry. The Holy Spirit certainly guides him in this. But man

must not put up obstacles. "The Spirit
too comes to help us in our weakness."

The simplest and most direct prayer to the Holy
Spirit is "Come Holy Spirit." An example of prayer
also worthy of use is: "Father, I put my life in your
hands. Jesus, I want to follow you. Holy Spirit, make
me wise and holy." Abandonment, discipleship, truth,
and love are the key ingredients of faithful prayer.

In Communion with Mary

In addition to the Trinity, our prayer as Catholics is
directed and in communion with Mary, the Mother of
God. The Catechism teaches: "In prayer the Holy Spirit
unites us to the person of the only Son, in his glorified humanity, through which and in which our prayer
unites us in the Church with the Mother of Jesus" (*CCC*
2673).

Mary, the Mother of God, shows us the way to her
Son. She always leads us to him. In our prayer to Mary
there are generally two movements: The first "magnifies" the Lord for the "great things" he has done for his
lowly servant and through her for all human beings.
The second movement entrusts the supplications and
praises of the children of God to the Mother of Jesus.
This twofold movement is exemplified in the great
Marian prayer—The Hail Mary.

Sentence by sentence, the Catechism analyzes the
Hail Mary—one of the most frequently recited prayers
in our treasury of prayers. We now focus on the Hail
Mary. It is, after all, the dominant prayer of the Rosary.
The totality of the Rosary is two hundred Hail Mary's.

Hail Mary. That is the greeting of the angel Gabriel. It is God himself, through the intermediary of an angel, who greets Mary. It is thus God's prayer. Regarding this angelic salutation, St. Louis de Montfort wrote:

> Since the salvation of mankind began through the *Hail Mary*, the salvation of each individual soul is linked up with this prayer. . . . It was this prayer which caused the Fruit of Life to spring up in this dry and barren world, and that it is this same prayer, devoutly said, which must cause the word of God to germinate in our souls, and to bear the Fruit of Life, Jesus Christ. . . . They speak of this prayer as a heavenly dew which seeps gently into the soil of the human soul, to bring forth fruit in due season.

To say "Hail Mary" brings us now into that mystical encounter between God and Mary. By our prayer, we unite ourselves with Mary at prayer and assume her worshipful spirit of humility, openness, and total self-donation. God took the initiative with Mary as he continues to do with us.

Full of grace, the Lord is with you. Mary is full of grace because the Lord is with her. God told her that, through the angel. The grace is the presence of God who is full of grace. It is as if "full of grace" were her name given by God. It is her essence, her identity, and the very meaning of her life.

Blessed are you among women and blessed is the fruit of your womb Jesus. Now we move to Elizabeth and her greeting. She is at the beginning of a long line of people who will call Mary blessed. Mary is blessed precisely because she believed. The entire posture of her life is an "obedience of faith"—not my will but your will be done. That is the essence of prayer—her prayer and every prayer. With regard to the name of Jesus, Archbishop Augustine DiNoia states, "Through Mary, then, we receive the Holy Name of Jesus by which the Lord manifests himself to us, hands himself over to us, and beckons us to know him personally and intimately."

Pray for us sinners, now and at the hour of our death. We acknowledge our sinfulness at the end of the prayer and pray that our Blessed Mother will be with us at the hour of our death as she was at the hour of her Son's death.

St. Louis de Montfort writes: "I have no more effective way of discovering whether a person is of God, than by enquiring whether he loves to say the Hail Mary." Urging further the daily recitation of the entire Rosary, the saint predicts: "At the moment of your death, you will bless the day and the hour when you paid heed to my advice; for, having sown in the blessings of Jesus and of Mary, you will reap eternal blessings in heaven."

Because of Mary's singular cooperation with the action of the Holy Spirit, the Church, moreover, loves to pray in communion with the Virgin Mary:

> Mary is the perfect *Orans* (pray-er), a figure of the Church. When we pray to her, we are adhering with her to the plan of the Father, who sends his Son to save all men. Like the beloved disciple we welcome Jesus' mother into our homes, for she has become the mother

of all the living. We can pray with and
to her. (*CCC* 2679)

Guides for Prayer

A Cloud of Witnesses

There are others, in addition to our Blessed Mother,
who make up the *living* tradition of prayer in the Church.
We are not alone. We are never alone. There is that great
"cloud of witnesses" who have preceded us into the
kingdom. The Church canonized some of them as saints;
others are known to us by their holiness. How is it that
those whom the Church recognized as saints "share in
the living tradition of prayer"?

The Catechism answers that question this way: "By
the example of their lives, the transmission of their writings, and their prayer today. . . . Their intercession is
their most exalted service to God's plan. We can and
should ask them to intercede for us and for the whole
world" (*CCC* 2683). Our prayer can profit from the rich
variety of spiritualities that exist in the Communion of
Saints (e.g., Benedictine, Dominican, Franciscan, Jesuit,
etc.). Each developed at a given time and responded to
the need of that time, and each has continued to this day.
The saints can be powerful intercessors in the living tradition of the Church. That is one reason why the Church
encourages couples to choose a saint's name for a child.

Servants of Prayer

There are many places where we receive guidance in prayer and the way to pray. First and foremost is the Christian family (the domestic Church)—the *first* place of education in prayer. In our own family home, we always said grace before meals, and we do it to this day. We always were taught to pray before bedtime—to pray for our parents and those in need. If a child does not learn to pray as a child, when will learning to pray happen? Will it in fact ever happen?

The Catechism also speaks of the responsibilities of ordained ministers and religious in teaching prayer. This cannot be underestimated. It speaks of spiritual directors and prayer groups. It speaks specifically of the catechesis of young people. The Catechism underscores that "the memorization of basic prayers offers an essential support to the life of prayer, but it is important to help learners savor their meaning" (CCC 2688). Sadly, I cannot tell you how many young people and young adults come to the Sacrament of Penance and do not know the Act of Contrition. As we continually encourage a regular use of that healing sacrament, it is important as well to encourage the learning of the Act of Contrition.

Places Favorable for Prayer

We can pray at any time of the day and at any place; yet there are some places more conducive to prayer than others. The Catechism mentions the church, God's house, as the proper place for liturgical prayer. It is also a wonderful place to adore the Blessed Sacrament reserved. I would agree with the Catechism's suggestion that we should cultivate a "prayer corner" in our homes where a copy of the scripture is prominently displayed. In our rectory we are blessed to have a chapel for meditation before the Blessed Sacrament. Parishes today likewise are providing more opportunities for people to pray in the presence of the Blessed Sacrament.

The Catechism also mentions pilgrimages that "evoke our earthly journey toward heaven and are traditionally very special occasions for renewal in prayer" (CCC 2691). Having led many pilgrimages, I can personally attest with enthusiasm that a pilgrimage can be a wonderful opportunity to learn about the saints of various countries, to pray in new forms and to deepen one's own prayer life, all the while enjoying each other's company at leisure.

With all of these guides to prayer, each of us should rejoice in the *living* Tradition of prayer in our Church— prayer that is at the heart of our relationship with Jesus Christ, his Father, and their Spirit.

A Witness to Prayer

As a child I learned that a sacrament "is a visible sign of an invisible grace." As an adult I have learned of the awesome graces associated with the Blessed Sacrament. When experiencing very difficult times in my life many years ago, I would go before the exposed Blessed Sacrament and beg God to help me get through that day, week, month. Over the years, through continued prayer (particularly devotion to the Blessed Sacrament), God answered my pleas. He filled my heart with peace, forgiveness, and trust in his healing powers. The Blessed Sacrament is the supreme source of supernatural graces. It's difficult to imagine life without this most Blessed Sacrament.

—Kelley Proxmire

Reflect

1. Who have been some of the teachers and models of prayer in your life? What did you learn from them?

2. How do you seek to cultivate an awareness of God throughout the day?

3. What place does the Blessed Mother have in your life of prayer?

Pray

Father, may I walk before you simply,
in faith, with humility, and with love.
I apply myself diligently to do nothing
and think nothing which may displease you.
I hope that when I have done what I can,
you will do with me what you please.

I give thanks for your great goodness
which I can never sufficiently express,
and for the many gifts you have given me
poor sinner as I am.
May all things praise you. Amen.

—adapted from the writings of
Brother Lawrence of the Resurrection

five

The Practicalities of Prayer

During the recently concluded Year for Priests, Pope Benedict XVI held up St. John Vianney, the nineteenth-century French Curé of Ars, as a model. I was struck by a passage from Vianney's *Catechetical Instructions* where he writes:

> Prayer is nothing else but union with God. When one has a heart that is pure and united with God, he is given a kind of serenity and sweetness that makes him ecstatic, a light that surrounds him with marvelous brightness. In this intimate union, God and the soul are fused together like two bits of wax that no one can ever pull apart. This union of God with a tiny creature is a lovely thing. It is happiness beyond understanding.

Stated another way, "Prayer is the life of the new heart" (*CCC* 2697). It is at the very core of being a follower of Jesus. At one level, prayer can be described as a heart-to-heart conversation with God. Mother Teresa reminds us, moreover, of the importance of silence in this conversation: "In silence he listens to us; in silence He speaks to our souls. In silence we are granted the privilege of listening to His voice" (*USCCA* 479–80).

Prayer is "the remembrance of God" (CCC 2697). Although the Catechism makes it clear that we are called to pray at *all* times, it importantly states that "we cannot pray 'at all times' if we do not pray at specific times, consciously willing it. These are the special times of Christian prayer, both in intensity and duration" (CCC 2697).

For sure, there are specific times each day when prayer is appropriate—morning and evening, before and after meals, on Sundays at Mass. But this does not happen automatically or simply. One must consciously choose to pray at these times. Just as with physical exercise, we must develop a discipline to our prayer and prayer times. There is, in fact, a certain rhythm about praying at specific times each day in a quiet place. Undoubtedly, it nourishes us and draws us closer to God. By no means does this mitigate our spontaneous prayer, our consciousness that the Lord always walks with us with his ear inclined toward us. In fact, cultivating an awareness of God's presence throughout the day allows the Lord to take over and do most of the work in our prayer. It is then more a question of our simply showing up at the appointed time and predisposing ourselves to his will for us.

The Expressions of Prayer

The Catechism lists three types (or expressions) of prayer—vocal, meditative, and contemplative. When the Gospel is read at Mass, we make the Sign of the Cross on our foreheads, lips, and hearts. We pray: "'May the Lord be in our minds, on our lips, and in our hearts.' Lips, minds, and hearts—these symbolize three kinds of prayer: vocal, meditative, and contemplative" (*USCCA* 473). Making the Sign of the Cross is an easy way to remember these three expressions of prayer.

Vocal Prayer

An obvious example of vocal prayer (prayer of our lips) would be the responses we make together at Mass. This is the form of prayer that is most readily accessible to us. We employ vocal prayer when, for example, we pray the Rosary together. It puts flesh onto our interior feelings. "We are body and spirit, and we experience the need to translate our feelings externally. We must pray with our whole being to give all power possible to our supplication" (*CCC* 2702). Jesus teaches us to say the most noteworthy of all vocal prayers—the Our Father. Jesus models vocal prayer himself at Gethsemane, the night before he died: "Abba. Father, all things are possible to you. Take this cup away from me, but not what I will but what you will" (Mk 14:36).

Meditative Prayer

Meditative Prayer (prayer of our minds) is above all a prayerful "quest" engaging thought, imagination, emotion, and desire. "This mobilization of faculties is necessary in order to deepen our convictions of faith, prompt the conversion of our heart, and strengthen our will to follow Christ" (*CCC* 2708). Although difficult to maintain, this form of prayer requires attentiveness. "The mind seeks to understand the why and how of the Christian life, in order to adhere and respond to what the Lord is asking" (CCC 2705). There are many good sources for meditation. Above all, of course, is the Holy Scripture—particularly the gospels. But, in addition, holy icons, liturgical texts of the day or season, writings of the spiritual fathers and works of spirituality may be used. Pope Benedict reminds us that "St Augustine compares meditation on the mysteries of God to the assimilation of food and uses a verb that recurs throughout the Christian tradition, 'to ruminate'; that is, the mysteries of God should continually resonate within us so that they become familiar to us, guide our lives and nourish us, as does the food we need to sustain us" (Audience, August 17, 2011).

How important it is thus to develop meditation in our prayer lives! In special fashion, listening to the Word of God each day helps us deepen our knowledge and love of our God! Otherwise we run the risk of becoming like the unproductive soil in the parable of the sower (Mk 4:15–19). Some seed (i.e., the Word) falls on the path: "As soon as they hear, Satan comes at once and takes away the word." When seeds are sown on rocky ground, "They hear the word, [they] receive it at once with joy. But they have no root; they last only for a time. Then when tribulation or persecution comes because of the word, they quickly fall away." Finally, some seed is sown among thorns: "They are the people who hear the word, but worldly anxiety, the lure of riches, and the craving for other things intrude and choke the word, and it bears no fruit."

When we meditate on a scripture text, we make it our own by confronting it with the reality of our own lives. We put ourselves in the gospel story. Under the influence of the Holy Spirit, we begin to identify with the characters and ask questions of ourselves. We begin to put on the mind and heart of Christ in a prayerful way. Lectio divina, the method of meditative reading developed by St. Benedict, is described more fully in chapter 4. At the end, however, the goal of Christian reflection is union with Jesus and the knowledge of the love of Jesus himself.

Contemplative Prayer

Perhaps the most difficult and yet the simplest form of prayer is contemplative prayer (prayer of our hearts). While it is difficult to clear our minds of all clutter, what is easy about this form of prayer is the total and clear focus on God alone. St. Teresa of Avila describes contemplative prayer as "nothing else than a close sharing between friends" (CCC 2709). "It is a gaze of faith fixed on Jesus" (CCC 2724). "It achieves real union with the prayer of Christ to the extent that it makes us share in his mystery" (CCC 2724). Contemplative prayer is the prayer of simple presence with one's lover. It can be intense. It is always recollected. It is the prayer of silent listening and love. "Contemplative prayer seeks him 'whom my soul loves'" (CCC 2709). One must consciously will time with the Lord. To do so requires a determined will and being recollected under the promptings of the Holy Spirit. It is our poor and loving surrender to the Lord. "'I look at him and he looks at me': this is what a certain peasant of Ars used to say to his holy curé about his prayer before the tabernacle" (CCC 2715). There can be no better place for contemplation than in the presence of the exposed Blessed Sacrament.

The Battle of Prayer

Whether our prayer is vocal, meditative, or contemplative, the Catechism acknowledges that prayer can be a struggle. In fact, it devotes a whole section to what it describes as "The Battle of Prayer."

You might ask, against whom is this battle? Quite simply, it is against ourselves and the wiles of the tempter, the evil one, the devil. It is certainly not in his interest that we develop a prayerful relationship with the Lord. Quite the contrary! The stakes are high for a follower of Jesus, for those of us who seek to live the Christian life faithfully.

"Prayer requires time, attention and effort" (*USCCA* 476). Prayer is not always easy—even for the saints. It is *both* a gift of grace *and* a determined response on our part. But so much often gets in the way. It might be that we simply do not feel liking praying. Perhaps we convince ourselves that we tried to pray but simply failed to experience God's presence. We easily give up and lose confidence. Each of us has these experiences from time to time. "The 'spiritual battle' of the Christian's new life is inseparable from the battle of prayer" (*CCC* 2725).

The Catechism is very pastorally sensitive and practical with respect to the components of the battle for *and* of prayer. At the outset, it states what prayer is not. It is not a psychological activity, nor is it an effort at concentration simply to fill a mental void. It is not merely a human effort. This is an implicit misconception on the part of each of us. Prayer is primarily the work of the Holy Spirit.

For some, the "mentality" of "this present world" can easily penetrate one's life, like a thief in the night. In this case, prayer is erroneously seen as an activity that can be considered true if verifiable by reason and science. Yet in reality "prayer is a mystery that overflows our conscious and unconscious lives" (*CCC* 2727). The bottom-line mentality also mistakenly turns the "success" of prayer into a profit-and-loss statement. Prayer being unproductive is seen as useless. Still others mistakenly see prayer as a "flight from the world in reaction against activism; but in fact, Christian prayer is neither an escape from reality nor a divorce from life" (*CCC* 2727).

> Finally, our battle has to confront what we experience as *failure in prayer*: discouragement during periods of dryness; sadness that, because we have "great possessions" we have not given all to the Lord; disappointment over not being heard according to our own will; wounded pride, stiffened by the indignity that is ours as sinners; our resistance to the idea that prayer is a free and unmerited gift; and so forth. The conclusion is always the same: what good does it do to pray? To overcome these obstacles, we must battle to gain humility, trust, and perseverance. (*CCC* 2728)

It is as if the Catechism writers were a part of each of our prayer lives. The Catechism specifies so clearly the two leading candidates for the difficulties that we experience in prayer—distraction and dryness.

We can draw hope from St. Thérèse of Lisieux, the Little Flower. In her autobiography, there is a passage about her experience of spiritual dryness that should give us some comfort. It is easy to forget that, even though she is always pictured with roses, she suffered terribly from tuberculosis, and she hemorrhaged a great deal. She writes:

> When my heart, weary of the envelop-ing darkness, tries to find some rest and strength in the thought of an everlasting life to come, my anguish only increases. It seems to me that the darkness itself, borrowing the voice of the unbeliever, cries mockingly, "You dream of a land of light and fragrance, you believe that the Creator of these wonders will be yours forever, you think to escape one day from the mists in which you now languish. Hope on! Hope on! Look for-ward to death! It will give you, not what you hope for, but a night darker still, the night of utter nothingness!"
>
> This description of what I suffer . . . is as far removed from reality as the painter's rough outline from the model he copies, but to write more might be to blaspheme . . . even now I may have said too much. May God forgive me! He knows how I try to live by faith, even though it affords me no consolation. I

have made more acts of faith during the
past year than in all the rest of my life.

Two Temptations

"Two frequent temptations threaten prayer: lack of
faith and acedia—a form of depression stemming from
lax ascetical practice that leads to discouragement"
(*CCC* 2755). We wonder: Is anyone listening? What if
I fail to get what I am praying for? Is he really there?
Yet I keep coming back to Jesus' response: "Without
me, you can do nothing" (Jn 15:5). The Catechism has
much to say about the two temptations of lack of faith
and acedia: "Some . . . stop praying because they think
their petition is not heard. Here two questions should
be asked: Why do we think our petition has not been
heard? How is our prayer heard, how is it 'efficacious'"
(*CCC* 2734)?

In answer to the first question, St. Augustine writes
in a letter to Proba:

> Why he should ask us to pray, when
> he knows what we need before we ask
> him, may perplex us if we do not realize
> that our Lord and God does not want
> to know what we want (for he cannot
> fail to know it) but wants us rather to
> exercise our desire through our prayers,
> so that we may be able to receive what
> he is preparing to give us. His gift is
> very great indeed, but our capacity is
> too small and limited to receive it.

The Catechism states further: "Do not be troubled if you do not immediately receive from God what you ask him; for he desires to do something even greater for you, while you cling to him in prayer" (*CCC* 2737).

With respect to the second concern, the "efficaciousness" of our prayer, we look to Jesus and our faith in him. It is, moreover, ultimately a matter of our faith, of our filial trust. It is the Holy Spirit of Jesus within us. "The prayer of Jesus makes Christian prayer an efficacious petition. He is its model, he prays in us and with us" (*CCC* 2740).

> Jesus also prays for us—in our place and on our behalf. All our petitions were gathered up, once for all, in his cry on the Cross and, in his Resurrection, heard by the Father. . . . If our prayer is resolutely united with that of Jesus, in trust and boldness as children, we obtain all that we ask in his name, even more than any particular thing: the Holy Spirit himself, who contains all gifts. (*CCC* 2741)

Ultimately, precisely because prayer is of the Holy Spirit, our challenge is simply to persevere in love. As the Catechism reminds us: "Against our dullness and laziness, the battle of prayer is that of humble, trusting, and persevering *love*" (*CCC* 2742). This is done even with all of the many obstacles to prayer and the temptations that get in our way. It requires, at the end, a yielding to the movement of the Holy Spirit within us.

In his book, *Paths to Prayer*, Bishop Robert F. Morneau writes:

> Prayer is not a luxury. It is more than a friendly invitation. Prayer is an imperative, a demand, a vital necessity. But our God never imposes a command without giving the necessary resources. Thus we are given the Holy Spirit who prays within us. One of the fundamental teachings of the Church is that we are temples of the Holy Spirit.

And "if we do not allow the Spirit to lead us, we fall back into the slavery of sin" (CCC 2744). Galatians 5:19–21 sets forth examples of this slavery which include immorality, impurity, licentiousness, idolatry, sorcery, hatreds, rivalry, jealousy, outbursts of fury, acts of selfishness, dissensions, factions, occasions of envy, drinking bouts, orgies, and the like.

In the end, prayer and Christian life cannot be separated:

> They concern the same love and the same renunciation, proceeding from love; the same filial and loving conformity with the Father's plan of love; the same transformation in the Holy Spirit who conforms us more and more to Christ Jesus; the same love for all men, the love with which Jesus has loved us. "Whatever you ask the Father in my name, he will give it to you. This I command you, to love one another." (CCC 2745)

Each of us lives in the desert of our busy lives. The perennial challenge for each of us is to be conscious of the Holy Spirit within us. That challenge means concretely listening to his voice in prayer. "Prayer is centered upon God. It is an emptying of oneself not for its own sake, but for the sake of being filled with God and entering into a deeper relationship with him" (*USCCA* 477). Despite the difficulties, the Holy Spirit will assuredly lead us through the desert. I know this from my own life. Hopefully each of us will find an oasis each day. That oasis is the living presence of God in our lives and it is there that we will concretely know him in our prayer and in his prayer with us.

A Witness to Prayer

I have attempted to pray seriously for about half of my life, but to be honest I usually feel like I am just beginning. Certainly, there are lots of kinds of prayers. As a priest I celebrate Holy Mass every day, which is the highest expression of prayer since it is the prayer of Christ himself. I say the Rosary every day and other vocal prayers, which are powerful and time-proven methods of prayer.

But where the rubber really meets the road is in mental prayer or meditation. I try to do an hour of mental prayer a day, but as Giles of Rome once remarked, sometimes it's like going to a dance and other times it's like going to war. Nevertheless, even when prayer seems like an uphill struggle, with distractions and dryness and interruptions, never once have I risen from my time in prayer and regretted that I "wasted" some time with

God. In fact, on days when I am praying—or trying to pray—everything seems to go smoother, my thoughts are more focused, my work more productive, my faith more intense, and my attitude more positive. Resolving to pray an hour a day—even, or especially, when "I don't have time"—has been the best decision of my life.

—Rev. Carter Griffin

Reflect

1. Which of these descriptions of prayer is the one that expresses your own prayer: union with God, the life of a new heart, a heart-to-heart conversation with God, listening to God's voice, remembrance of God?

2. Which form of prayer are you most comfortable with: vocal prayer, meditative prayer, or contemplative prayer? Why do you think this is so? What place do the other forms of prayer have in your life?

3. Does the image of prayer as a battle reflect your experience? How do you deal with distractions in prayer? How do you handle discouragement?

Pray

Let nothing disturb you,
Let nothing frighten you,
All things are passing away:

God never changes.
Patience obtains all things.
Whoever has God lacks nothing;
God alone suffices.

—St. Teresa of Avila

s i x

The Prayer of Jesus
on Holy Thursday

Jesus is our model of how to pray. In this chapter, we look at some of the most intensely personal prayers that Jesus left us. On the night before he died, Jesus prayed in the upper room for his disciples and for us. During his agony in the Garden of Gethsemane, Jesus prayed to his Father. And on the cross Jesus prayed again to the Father and left us Seven Last Words, (the focus of chapter 7). In the upper room, in the garden, and on the hill called Calvary, it is as if we were eavesdropping on the very personal prayer of Jesus. It provides a powerful insight into his very prayer.

The Prayer in the Upper Room

At the conclusion of Jesus' farewell address to his disciples (chapters 14 to 17 of John's gospel) is the sublime prayer called the "priestly" prayer of Jesus (*CCC* 2747). His farewell address is the longest prayer transmitted in any of the gospels. At the end of the Last Supper, Jesus and his disciples stand and raise their eyes in the traditional Jewish way. Jesus prays to the Father, to Abba, "Father, the hour has come" (Jn 17:1).

Yes, it is the "hour," the long-awaited hour, the hour of his death toward which his entire mission was directed. It is the hour in which God's glory is to be supremely revealed. Immediately before leaving the upper room for Gethsemane, he prays for himself, for his disciples, and for those who will follow him—for you and me. In Jesus, we have the high priest, as a representative of all humanity, presenting these prayers of petition and intercession to his Father.

First, he prayed for himself as he faced the cross (Jn 17:1–5). "Now glorify me, Father, with you, with the glory that I had with you before the world began" (Jn 17:5). In a word, Jesus prays that God will crown the work that he undertook at the Father's command (i.e., that God will glorify him as he prepares to meet his death out of love for us).

Second, he prayed for his disciples (Jn 17:6–19). "I pray for them. I do not pray for the world but for the ones you have given me, because they are yours" (Jn 17:9). He asks the Father to protect them, as he will no longer be with them. He prays that they may share the joy that he and the Father share. He asks the Father to "keep them from the evil one." He prays that they may be consecrated in truth (i.e., made fit for divine service, as Jesus prepares for his sacrificial offering on the cross).

Finally, he prays for all believers yet to come (Jn 17:20–23). How comforting it is to know that Jesus actually prayed for you and me at the Last Supper! "I pray not only for them [his disciples], but also for those who will believe in me through their word" (Jn 17:20). He speaks of those who believe in him, based on the word of his disciples—that vital contact with subsequent generations. That is also Jesus' prayer.

The priestly, or intercessory, prayer of Jesus is the "prayer of our high priest, inseparable from his sacrifice, from his passing over (Passover) to the Father to whom he is wholly 'consecrated'" (*CCC* 2747). From this prayer, Jesus was to go straight to his betrayal, trial, and ultimately the cross. He would not speak to his disciples again until the cross. In a real sense, his prayer was not one of despair, but a prayer of glory. "And I have given them the glory you gave me, so that they may be one, as we are one, I in them and you in me, that they may be brought to perfection as one, that the world may know that you sent me, and that you loved them even as you loved me" (Jn 17:22–23).

The Prayer in the Garden

It was night. After the Last Supper, Jesus retired with Peter, James, and John, and his disciples to the Mount of Olives and the Garden of Gethsemane. Three accounts from the synoptic gospels (Mt 26:36–46; Mk 14:32–42; and Lk 22:39–46), in addition to a short account from John 12:27–28, describe what happened there (cf. *CCC* 612).

Upon arriving, he told his disciples: "Sit here while I pray" (Mk 14:32). It was a night of prayer. It was his final night of prayer. Jesus often prayed at night. Matthew tells us that he "fell prostrate in prayer, saying, 'My Father, if it is possible, let this cup pass from me; yet, not as I will, but as you will'" (Mt 26:39). In Mark, we learn that "he advanced a little and fell to the ground and prayed that if it were possible the hour might pass

by him; he said, 'Abba, Father, all things are possible to
you. Take this cup away from me, but not what I will but
what you will'" (Mk 14:35–36). It was a night of anguish,
a night when he struggled prayerfully with his will and
the will of his Father. This prayer rests at the heart of
the Our Father, appropriated by Jesus in the darkness of
that night. Jesus was troubled and distressed and fearful
and alone with his Father. At its deepest level, he experienced the loneliness of the human condition. Recalling
Psalm 43:5, a psalm he had to have known well, Jesus
prays, "My soul is sorrowful even to death" (Mk 14:34).
Death was imminent.

Pope Benedict XVI describes so well the prayer of
Gethsemane as an internal struggle for Jesus:

> The two parts of Jesus' prayer are pre-
> sented as the confrontation between two
> wills: there is the "natural will" of the
> man Jesus, which resists the appalling
> destructiveness of what is happening
> and wants to plead that the chalice pass
> from him; and there is the "filial will"
> that abandons itself totally to the father's
> will. In order to understand this mystery
> of the "two wills" as much as possible, it
> is helpful to take a look at John's version
> of the prayer. Here, too, we find the same
> two prayers on Jesus' lips: "Father, save
> me from this hour . . . Father, glorify your
> name." (Jn 12:27–28)

In the end, Pope Benedict concludes: "Jesus uttered
both prayers, but the first one, asking for deliver-
ance, merges into the second one, asking for God to be

glorified by the fulfillment of his will—and so the conflicting elements blend into unity deep within the heart of Jesus' human existence." Or as Blessed John Paul II has written: "The words of that prayer of Christ in Gethsemane prove *the truth of love through the truth of suffering*" (*SD* 18).

In our own prayer, we seek also to abandon ourselves to the will of the Father. So often, we pray "thy will be done." There can be no better model than the Gethsemane prayer of Jesus on the night before he died.

Gethsemane also represents the desire of Our Lord Jesus that we pray "with" him. Three times, unsuccessfully, he returned to his disciples and asked them to watch with him in prayer. In his invitation for them to pray with him, it was as if he were reciting the doxology at the end of the Eucharistic Prayer at Mass and applying it to himself—"through him, and with him, and in him." Do we pray with Christ, in Christ, and with Christ as members of his living body? Are we similarly and often asleep at the wheel? Do we hear the words of Jesus: "Why are you sleeping? Get up and pray that you may not undergo the test" (Lk 22:46)?

St. Thomas More's last work, *The Sadness of Christ*, written in the Tower of London as he was preparing to die, is a reflection in large part on Jesus' agony in the garden and More's identification with him. For example, More writes: "To those whose hearts are troubled, meditation on this agony provides great consolation, and rightly so, since it was for this very purpose—to console the afflicted—that our Savior in his kindness made known his own affliction, which no one else knew or could have known."

And with respect to prayer, the heart of his agony in the garden, More writes: "Since our Savior Christ saw that nothing is more profitable than prayer . . . he decided to take this opportunity, on the way to his death, to reinforce his teaching by his words and example and to put the finishing touches on this most necessary point just as he did on the other parts of his teaching." Having prayed, Jesus was thus able to say with humble confidence that "the hour has come. Behold, the Son of Man is to be handed over to sinners" (Mk 14:41). His betrayer was at hand.

A Witness to Prayer

I have been attracted to prayer since I was a child growing up in a good but not very pious Catholic family. My prayer life has been shaped by Catholic liturgical prayer, education, meeting holy people, learning to meditate, and by the decisions and sufferings of ordinary life. Personal prayer changes as we grow in faith and opens our living space by keeping us aware of the eternal promise of Christ— that we will live with him forever. The Church's sacraments, especially Eucharist and Penance, fill us with Christ's life now. Prayer is the grace of communication with our loving God, bringing us the living water of God's life without which our efforts to live a life of virtue wither on the vine. Prayer is part of my daily life and affects all of my other relationships and choices. Perhaps it is God's chisel, forming the new person out of the old block of marble the way Michelangelo once said a block of marble hides the concept living in the artist's mind. Prayer allows God

to make a new creation out of us, which will only
be revealed in heaven. That thought makes me very
happy.

—Mary Ellen Bork

Reflect

1. Often we think of our prayer as something we
   do alone and direct to Jesus. What difference
   does it make for you to consider that when you
   pray Jesus is praying with you?

2. What does it mean for you to say, as Jesus did,
   "Thy will be done"?

Pray

Father,
I abandon myself into your hands; do with me
what you will.
Whatever you may do, I thank you:
I am ready for all, I accept all.
Let only your will be done in me, and in all your
creatures.
I wish no more than this, O Lord.

Into your hands I commend my soul;
I offer it to you
with all the love of my heart,
for I love you, Lord,
and so need to give myself,
to surrender myself into your hands,

without reserve,
and with boundless confidence,
for you are my Father.

—Charles de Foucauld

seven

The Prayer of Jesus
from the Cross

In his second book on Jesus, a book titled *Jesus of Nazareth, Holy Week: From the Entrance into Jerusalem to the Resurrection*, Pope Benedict XVI writes poignantly of the cross of Jesus:

> The Cross is his throne, from which he draws the world to himself. From this place of total self-sacrifice, from this place of truly divine love, he reigns as the true king in his own way—a way that neither Pilate nor the members of the Sanhedrin had been able to comprehend.

The focus of this chapter is what Jesus said as he hung dying on the cross. His words from the cross give meaning and credibility to his ascent to Jerusalem. In so doing, Jesus proceeds to the ultimate revelation of the cross, the resurrection, and the sending of the Holy Spirit. He goes with prayer on his lips.

> When the hour had come for him to fulfill the Father's plan of love, Jesus allows a glimpse of the boundless depth of his filial prayer, not only before he

> freely delivered himself up ("Abba . . .
> not my will, but yours."), but even in his
> last words on the Cross, where prayer
> and the gift of self are but one: "Father,
> forgive them, for they know not what
> they do"; "Truly, I say to you, today you
> will be with me in Paradise"; "Woman,
> behold your son. . . . Behold your moth-
> er"; "I thirst"; "My God, My God, why
> have your forsaken me?" "It is finished";
> "Father, into your hands I commit my
> spirit!" until the "loud cry" as he expires,
> giving up his spirit. (*CCC* 2605)

Jesus simultaneously speaks and acts from the pulpit of the cross in a most moving way. Precisely in the
midst of his terrible pain and suffering, *the* deed of his
whole life, his crucifixion, the supreme act of unself-
ish love, Jesus speaks. From the pulpit of the cross, his
words give lasting credibility to this wondrous act of
love. They are words of prayer. It is, moreover, a deed
of incredible love. In effect, he acted out his teaching
on the cross in a concrete way and revealed his wondrous love for us at the same time. His words were not
unlike a sacred commentary on what he was doing for
us on Golgotha. As Blessed John Paul II has written:
"In bringing about the Redemption through suffering,
Christ *has also raised human suffering to the level of the
Redemption*" (*SD* 19). In so doing, we hear his words of
prayer, words from the Hebrew psalms, words of communion with his Father Abba, words of communion
and solidarity with and for others to hear, words for
us to hear over and over again, and words we cannot ever tire of hearing. They are words which create

an environment of faith, hope, and love amid what otherwise would simply be a scene of horror, extreme brutality, and human perversity in its ugliest form.

They are called his Seven Last Words, or described by some as his "seven sets of words." In preaching the Seven Last Words of Christ throughout my years of priesthood each Good Friday, I have been greatly inspired in particular by three books on this subject and they are reflected in this chapter. Their authors include Father Alfred McBride, O. Praem.; Dominican Father Romanus Cessario; and Archbishop Fulton J. Sheen. In addition, I have relied on Pope Benedict XVI's first encyclical *God Is Love* (*Deus Caritas Est*) and his book *Jesus of Nazareth, Holy Week: From the Entrance into Jerusalem to the Resurrection.*

The First Word

"Father, forgive them, they know not what they do."

They had scourged him and lacerated his body. They had put a crown of thorns on his head. They had insulted him and made fun of him. They were now nailing him to a tree. There was the flush of a fever mixed with the chill of his fast approaching death. It was, if you will, a seemingly incredible example of man's inhumanity against man—an example of what we have seen and continue to see so often in our own world—particularly in the last century. The twentieth century was a century that produced the Battle of the Bulge, Normandy, Auschwitz (referred to in a Vatican document on the Shoah as "an unspeakable tragedy"), the Tet Offensive, Bosnia, and the awful slaughters in

Africa. Now in the twenty-first century, the names of Iraq, Afghanistan, Libya and the Arab Spring conjure up violence and death as well. We will never forget 9/11, nor should we forget the millions of pre-born babies being deprived of life in the womb. And yet, on Golgotha—Scull Hill—this inhumanity is being done to our God, a God who becomes crucified. And through the ages, many have and will continue to reject his redemptive love, the price he paid out of love for us.

Punctuating this evil and cruel drama, we hear the voice, his prayerful voice, a voice of divine generosity which is so very consoling—"Father, forgive them, they know not what they do." It is as if the words of Jesus in Matthew 18:21, to forgive not simply seven times, but seven times seventy times, take on new vitality, new meaning, new credibility. Or the words of the Our Father, "Forgive us our trespasses *as* we forgive those who trespass against us," make more and more sense. Jesus now witnesses to his own teaching in the midst of his awful suffering on the wood of the cross. His first word is not only a teaching, it is a prayerful act of forgiveness. It was a terrible scene, yet one permeated with a haunting beauty which came forth from the magnificent love of his forgiving and pierced heart.

And he forgave them because of their ignorance. What profound ignorance to pin our God to a tree! And yet the wound of ignorance results from original sin. In his book *Jesus of Nazareth, Holy Week: From the Entrance into Jerusalem to the Resurrection*, Pope Benedict asks: "Are we not blind precisely as people with knowledge? . . . Ignorance diminishes guilt, and it leaves open the path to conversion. . . . The Lord makes their ignorance the motive for his pleas for forgiveness: he sees it as a door that can open us to conversion."

The Catechism describes original sin as "a sin 'contracted' and not 'committed'—a state and not an act" (*CCC* 404). It is the same wound, a wound caused by the sin of Adam that brought Jesus to the cross. He suffered and died for that wound to be healed. Is ignorance not the cause of so much of our sin, our crime, and our inability to love in our world? Sin—crying out for forgiveness and healing!

Jesus gives us a most credible example of how to deal with the root cause of ignorance, the sin of ignorance. It is to turn the other cheek, even when one is suffering, precisely as one hangs dying on the wood of the cross. Yes, our crosses also so often reflect his crucified figure, silhouetted against the darkening skies of our lives.

Were there ever words so receptive to the ears of those burdened down by sin and alienation and guilt? In each of our lives, there are things, actions, attitudes, and people that need forgiving. If only we could listen to the words of Jesus who forgives his persecutors and who also forgives us. Then we too would look again at the power of forgiveness in our lives—perhaps that one troubling relationship or that one sin—lots of things to be forgiven and to forgive. Dominican Father Romanus Cessario writes: "Those impervious to sin remain impervious also to forgiveness." That need not be.

The Second Word

*"Amen, I say to you, today you will
be with me in paradise."*

It is not surprising that Jesus dies between two thieves nor that he spends his last hours between two lost sheep. It is precisely the lost sheep that Jesus came to save. One was angry and made a sarcastic remark to Jesus. The other, we call him Dismas, captures our special attention when he asked Jesus for salvation: "Jesus, remember me when you come into your kingdom" (Lk 23:42).

Archbishop Fulton J. Sheen writes: "One would have thought a saint would have been the first soul purchased over the counter of Calvary by the red coins of redemption, but in the Divine plan it is a thief who steals that privilege and marches as the escort of the king of kings into Paradise."

The scene is dramatic: three crosses. Jesus' death between two of them dramatically signifies his solidarity with the "world of human suffering." It is a profound solidarity with our personal suffering whatever it might be, suffering unique to each of us, physical or mental. Perhaps it is the terrible hurt of a broken marriage, the agony of a drawn-out terminal illness, psychological disease, the sufferings of millions under the burden of old age, the estimated 5.5 million children in our country under the age of twelve who are hungry or another six million who are underfed. The world of human suffering also includes the nearly eight hundred million people around the globe who suffer from hunger and malnutrition—all of this at the beginning of the twenty-first century. Yet Jesus does not suffer alone, but with two thieves, with each of us.

Christian behavior, the example of an innocent one going to slaughter, is a silent, effective, and powerful proclamation of the Good News. It is wordless witness. It is Jesus' kind of witness.

Such witness uniquely triggers the power of conversion. It is never too late for any of us. Dismas's conversion is akin to a deathbed conversion. "Jesus, remember me." It is never too late to embrace the gospel and repent. His word gives us hope: "*Today*, you will be with me in Paradise" (Lk 23:43). How it echoes the urgency of Jesus' first words in the synagogue at Nazareth as he began his public ministry: "*Today* this scripture passage is fulfilled in your hearing" (Lk 4:21). The second word of Jesus from the cross is as much about Dismas as what was said by Jesus. Seeing Jesus, the innocent one, Dismas must have developed a silent bond of affection for him. He felt the need for spiritual life and Jesus satisfied that need by the power and humility of his obedient suffering. Dismas experienced a religious conversion on the cross.

Do we give witness to the love of Jesus in our families, in our workplaces, with our friends, with those we meet? One never knows where such witness of love can have a spiritual and lasting effect. Who would have thought that one would experience conversion in the midst of dying on a cross? Jesus' second word reassures us and encourages us never to give up our efforts at strong, moral, and courageous Christian example. As Pope Paul VI wrote in the apostolic exhortation, *Evangelization in the Modern World*: "Modern man listens more willingly to witnesses than to teachers, and

if he does listen to teachers, it is because they are witnesses" (*EN* 41).

I invite you to ponder how it was that Jesus evan-
gelized from the cross precisely in the midst of his
suffering. It is a lasting model for you and me. This
is the stuff of true, effective, courageous, and humble
evangelization.

The Third Word

"Woman, behold your son. . . . Behold your mother."

When Jesus saw his mother and the disciple there
whom he loved, he said to his mother, "Woman, behold
your son." Then he said to the disciple, "Behold your
mother."

Woman is the same word that Jesus used at the
wedding feast of Cana. Unlike the word *mother*, which
would imply only her physical parentage, the use of
woman both at Cana and at the foot of the cross, both
recorded by St. John, speaks to Mary's unique and
mysterious maternal role in the history of salvation. It
is her role at Bethlehem, Cana, Calvary, and finally in
the upper room on Pentecost at the birth of the Church.

At Cana, the beginning of his public ministry, Mary
invited Jesus to save a newly married couple from a
potentially terrible embarrassment. More importantly,
she invited him to begin his saving work by changing
water into wine that he might manifest his glory. Now
she was present at the foot of the cross as his saving
work was being brought to its conclusion. His hour
had come and his mother was there.

Stabat Mater. Mary, the Mother, stands at the foot of the cross. There, too, are John, the beloved disciple, and other relatives and friends. The cross challenged her to let go in a way she could never have anticipated. No mother ever wants to see her son die. Mary must have felt the wounds and suffering of her Son as if they were her own. Jesus, in contrast, was concerned about the care of his mother. He was concerned about the care of his Church, his living body. He was concerned about each of us.

The words uttered by Jesus from the cross signify that the motherhood of her who bore Christ finds a new continuation in the Church and through the Church. The Church, each one of us baptized into him, is symbolized and represented by John who is told, "Behold your mother." Mary is our Mother, too. As the Catechism teaches: "Jesus desires to associate with his redeeming sacrifice those who were to be its first beneficiaries. This is achieved supremely in the case of his mother, who was associated more intimately than any other person in the mystery of his redemptive suffering" (CCC 618).

Stabat Mater. Mary stands at the foot of the cross. And Mary prays in the upper room at Pentecost. Mary is a woman of deep faith, a faith that never faltered. Mary is also a woman who never ceases praying, communicating with God, praying for each of us as a mother does for her child. She is a powerful intercessor. We can never forget the beautiful words of the Memorare: "Never was it known that anyone who fled to thy protection, implored thy help, or sought thy intercession was left unaided."

No other human being in history spent more years, days, and hours in such personal proximity to Jesus than Mary, from birth until his death on a cross. How close are we to Jesus? Are we with him only in the good times, or do we stand by him when we experience the pains and suffering of our crosses?

The Fourth Word

"My God, my God, why have you forsaken me?"

Even with his mother and dearest friends close to his side, an overwhelming sense of abandonment, isolation, and loneliness overcame Jesus. Above all, he felt the absence of God's presence. That emptiness, when God is not in our lives, or so it seems, can cause terrible pain for us as well. It had to have been the most crucifying of all pain for Jesus. How he, who was God, could know such abandonment, such emptiness, we do not know. We do know from St. Paul that "he emptied himself, taking the form of a slave, being born in the likeness of men" (Phil 2:7). He took on our human condition. He emptied himself to that point where even the presence of God is denied him. That is the ultimate emptying. These words reveal that most poignantly from the cross. Or as Benedict XVI writes: "It is no ordinary cry of abandonment. Jesus is praying the great psalm of suffering Israel, and so he is taking upon himself all the tribulation, not just of Israel, but of all those in this world who suffer from God's concealment."

But what does Jesus do at that moment?

He turns to prayer. Specifically, he turns to Psalm 22 in his hour of abandonment. He prays the first line of that psalm—"My God, my God, why have you forsaken me?" Jesus prayed from the cross this Hebrew psalm. By choosing to pray these words out loud, Jesus reveals how much he had integrated that Hebrew prayer into his own life. Pope Benedict XVI reminds us:

> Yet when Jesus utters the opening words of the psalm, the whole of this great prayer is essentially already present—including the certainty of an answer to prayer, to be revealed in the Resurrection. . . . The cry of extreme anguish is at the same time the certainty of an answer from God, the certainty of salvation—not only for Jesus himself, but for "many."

That means it is a model for each one of us as well.

It is a model for us when we find ourselves in the same situation, as we so often do, when we feel abandoned, lonely, isolated, suffering from a lack of love, yes even the lack of the presence of God. He is, nevertheless, always with us. "And behold, I am with you always, until the end of the age" (Mt 28:20).

The phenomenon of spiritual aridity is not uncommon, even among those of us who regularly seek him in prayer with a humble heart. Jesus has not abandoned us. More likely, we have abandoned him. In those situations, it is time to look more closely to Jesus on the cross. It is time to listen to his fourth word from the cross and identify with him who so clearly identified with us. His darkest moment, and ours, is one darkness.

And yet, in that darkest hour, Jesus did not give up discouraged. Nor should we. He was basically telling God: I want to feel your presence. He did not let his desolation absorb him in self-pity. He chose instead to continue to submit obediently to the Father's will. There is a momentum to the work of salvation. As he prayed that psalm, the last invocation of Psalm 22, "May your hearts be ever merry!" seemed to stir in him already the smell of the Easter lily, a scent that should always be with us at every moment and hour of the day. Father Romanus Cessario reminds us that it is as if he wanted to reassure us "beyond all doubt that, whatever dark sentiments may envelop our hearts and minds, nothing can 'separate us from the love of God'" (Rom 8:39). Or speaking of the fourth word, Pope Benedict XVI writes in *Deus Caritas Est:* "Immersed like everyone else in the dramatic complexity of historical events [each of us remains] unshakably certain that God is our Father and loves us, even when his silence remains incomprehensible" (*DCE* 38).

The Fifth Word

"I thirst."

Nobertine Father Alfred McBride reminds us that: "Heavy blood loss causes severe dehydration. The scourging at the pillar and the crowning with thorns is the reason for Jesus' physical thirst." It is important to meditate on the suffering and blood-letting that

Jesus endured for us. By your own blood, O Jesus, you brought us back to God!

He shed much blood for us beginning with the scourging at the pillar. As the soldiers repeatedly struck Jesus' back with full force, the iron balls caused deep contusions. He was severely whipped. And the crowning with thorns, in effect a cap of thorns covering his whole head, caused his head to bleed profusely. Amused that this weakened man had claimed to be a king, the soldiers began to mock him by placing a robe on his shoulders and a crown on his head. A major cause of his physical thirst, that brutal scourging and crowning, evidences dramatically what Jesus would undergo to make the everlasting covenant of love with us possible. His battered figure is an everlasting reminder that to live is to love, and that to love involves not only joy, but also suffering. Oh how precious and life–giving is the blood of Jesus! "Take this, all of you, and drink from it, this is the chalice of my blood, the blood of the new and everlasting covenant, which will be poured out for you and for many for the forgiveness of sins."

It is the same blood that Jesus shed during his passion, this same blood, his blood that heals our sins. Every time we confess our sins in confession, we are covered with the life-giving blood of Jesus poured out for us in the scourging, the crowning, and ultimately the crucifixion. How can we not confess our sins, even our little sins, and confess them regularly and encourage others to confess in sacramental confession?

This loss of blood caused Jesus to be thirsty. But there is a deeper cause of his thirst. It is the reason for his whole life, his whole ministry that found its fulfillment on the cross. Jesus thirsts for each one of us. It rests at the heart of his ministry. Jesus had a desire and thirst for souls. This is the key to this fifth word from the cross. Even from the cross, particularly from the cross, Jesus reminds us of his thirst for us.

The physical thirst, realistic as it was, is but a sign of a deeper thirst. It is the thirst to be able to give God's most precious gift to us, his love, a share in his wonderful life. The words "I thirst" are the most personal and intimate of all the words from the cross precisely because they speak to each of us—to those of us who seek him regularly and to those who reject and despise him.

In our pain, in the pain that life gives us from time to time, we are challenged to focus on the love-thirst of Jesus. It is a thirsting love revealed from the midst of his suffering and pain on the cross. It was a thirst for each of us that was so important to him. So must ours be for those individuals he puts in our path. This is a time to recoup some of that wonderful zeal for souls, particularly those souls close to us but seemingly far away from the Lord Jesus. That zeal and thirst must be at the core of our Christian existence. "My being thirsts for God, the living God. When can I go and see the face of God?" (Ps 42:3).

The Sixth Word

"It is finished."

Consummatum est. It is finished. It is achieved. It is completed. His hour had finally come. The hour that had not arrived at Cana, at a wedding feast, arrived at

Golgotha. It arrived instead on a cross, a wedding of reconciliation between God and each one of us forever. Yes, the will of his Father was completed. It was to restore in the second Adam, Jesus, what had been lost by the first Adam. Seemingly defeated, he was in actuality the conqueror. In the words of Archbishop Fulton J. Sheen, in saying it is consummated, Jesus means:

> He has finished the foundation; we must build upon it. He has finished the ark, opening His side with a spear and clothing Himself in the garment of His precious blood, but we must enter the ark. He stands at the door and knocks, but the latch is on the inside, and only we can open it. He has enacted the consecration, but the communion depends on us; and whether our work will ever be finished depends entirely on how we relive His life and become other Christs, for His Good Friday and His passion avails us nothing unless we take up His Cross and follow Him.

Consummatum est. As Father Alfred McBride writes: "On the cross, he made a bread offering of his broken body. . . . He seemed like the loaf of sacrificial bread burnt and transformed into a new reality. On the cross, Jesus' body of death was becoming the Bread of Life."

By the sacrifice on the cross of his body and the shedding of his blood, Jesus effected that sacrificial meal that recalls and makes present his passion, death, and resurrection. It was celebrated at the Last Supper and continues in the Eucharist each second of every

day somewhere in the world. This saving act was a
supreme act of sacrificial love for us. It lies at the heart
of our faith. What wondrous love Jesus gives us at
Mass, the Sacrament of Love. How can we live without
the Eucharist, the great gift of Calvary!

On the cross, Jesus has profoundly touched our
human experience. To this day, the image and likeness
of our God will forever be seen in children distorted by
hunger, in men and women disfigured by torture and
war, in the destruction of human life, particularly the
most defenseless, the pre-born and the helpless elderly.

The fruits of his passion and death continue
through signs and words in our day, above all in the
Eucharist, but also in that special anointing, the Sacrament of the Sick. It is the sacrament that unites us, in
special fashion, with the passion of Christ. The Catechism states:

> By the grace of this sacrament the sick
> person receives the strength and the
> gift of uniting himself more closely to
> Christ's Passion: in a certain way he is
> consecrated to bear fruit by configura-
> tion to the Savior's redemptive Passion.
> Suffering, a consequence of original sin,
> acquires a new meaning; it becomes
> a participation in the saving work of
> Jesus. (CCC 1521)

On the cross, Jesus leads us from darkness to light,
from death to a new and better life, to a life of which
there is no end and where the desires of all human
beings are finally and completely fulfilled. For such is

his work completed and brought to perfection. *Consummatum est.*

The Seventh Word

"Father, into your hands I commend my spirit."

At the time of final surrender, the surrender of his spirit, Jesus again turns in prayer to a Hebrew psalm, a psalm that his mother must have taught him as a child. From Psalm 31, he prays: "Into your hands I commend my spirit." This night prayer taught to the child Jesus thus becomes his final prayer. It is his prayer on the threshold of his Father's house.

That final prayer has been the prayer of many saints and martyrs throughout the ages. It is the prayer of countless men and women who have died with the name of Jesus on their lips and in their hearts and minds. It has been said by parents mourning the unexpected death of a young child, by married couples broken by divorce, by men and women whose lives are marked by love and patience in the face of the most trying circumstances. It is the prayer of peaceful surrender to the God who made us and the Christ who redeemed us on the wood of the cross.

In his beautiful encyclical on the Church's teaching on morality, *The Splendor of Truth,* Blessed John Paul II spoke of martyrdom as an outstanding sign of holiness in the Church (*VS* 93). Understood as bearing witness after the example of Jesus' total surrender on the cross, the martyrs went to their death shedding their blood because of the power of the living truth within them.

Understood as bearing witness, testifying to the truth about Jesus, particularly to his obedient surren- der to his Father on the cross, martyrdom does not always end in the shedding of blood.

You and I, after the example of Jesus on the cross and empowered by the living power of his cross, are called each day in our walk with Jesus to be martyrs for the faith. We are called, moreover, to be witnesses of the faith "which is a lived knowledge of Christ, a living remembrance of his commandments, and a *truth to be lived out*," even at the cost of suffering and grave sacrifice (*VS* 88). It is the call to a holy life, a call that will lead to a holy death and life eternal.

A Witness to Prayer

Prayer for me is attentive listening to presence, the presence of the Lord. It begins with morning prayer, both personal and liturgical. This sets the tone for quiet attentiveness to Jesus in ordinary daily activities. Without this daily nourishment of the Eucharist, the Rosary, and a contemplative attitude of listening, the anxieties and distractions of our fast-paced world tend to take over. Evening prayer and spiritual reading once again restore the peace that "surpasseth understanding."

—Mary Shivanandan

Reflect

1. Jesus' words and actions on the cross are in perfect harmony. Reflect on those people— perhaps some whom you have known, some who may be saints or otherwise well known— whose faith in the midst of suffering spoke powerfully to you. How would you connect their witness to one of Christ's Seven Last Words?

2. In your own life, which of Christ's Seven Last Words expresses best his invitation to you to unite your sufferings with his own?

3. In what ways have you experienced the presence of Mary as a faithful mother who stands with you in suffering? How could you invite Mary more fully into your life to be that support?

Pray

Stabat Mater

At the Cross her station keeping,
stood the mournful Mother weeping,
close to her son to the last.

Through her heart, His sorrow sharing,
all His bitter anguish bearing,
now at length the sword has passed.

O how sad and sore distressed
was that Mother, highly blest,
of the sole-begotten One.

Christ above in torment hangs,
she beneath beholds the pangs
of her dying glorious Son.

Is there one who would not weep,
whelmed in miseries so deep,
Christ's dear Mother to behold?

—Fifteenth Century
Translated by Edward Caswall

eight

The Rosary

Inevitably, after daily Mass in many parishes throughout the world, there is a faithful group of parishioners who recite the rosary aloud. This daily devotion is a powerful witness that subtly, for sure, affects the spiritual lives of each and every parish priest and deepens the life of the parish. The sound of this prayer resonates in our priestly hearts even if we are unable to join those holy men and women as they pray. The rosary is, after all, a powerful and enduring example of the unique and lasting devotion to Mary that rests in the very heart of the Church. It is a prayer loved by so many priests, consecrated women and men, and laity alike and represents Mary's particular role in our lives. "Simple yet profound, it still remains, at the dawn of this third millennium, a prayer of great significance, destined to bring forth a harvest of holiness" (*RVM* 1).

> The popularity of the Rosary has been attributed to St. Dominic (1170–1221) and the Dominican Order. It grew out of the laity's desire to have 150 prayers to match the 150 psalms chanted by monks in monasteries. In 1569, St. Pius V officially recommended the praying "of 150

103

> angelic salutations . . . with the Lord's
> prayer at each decade . . . while med-
> itating on the mysteries which recall
> the entire life of our Lord Jesus Christ."
> (*USCCA* 298)

The mysteries of the Rosary focus on the events in the life of Christ. The Rosary is, at its heart, a prayerful way to holiness and a useful way to stay close to Christ through the intercession of his Mother Mary. Tradition-ally, they include the Joyful Mysteries (the Annuncia-tion, the Visitation, the Nativity, the Presentation of Jesus in the Temple, and the Finding of the Child Jesus after Three Days in the Temple); the Sorrowful Mys-teries (the Agony in the Garden, the Scourging at the Pillar, the Crowning with Thorns, the Carrying of the Cross, and the Crucifixion and Death of Jesus); and the Glorious Mysteries (the Resurrection, the Ascen-sion into Heaven, the Sending of the Holy Spirit upon the Apostles at Pentecost, the Assumption of Mary, and the Crowning of Mary as Queen of Heaven and Earth).

On October 16, 2002, Blessed John Paul II published an apostolic letter titled *The Rosary of the Virgin Mary (Rosarium Virginis Mariae)*. In that document, he added five additional mysteries that he called the Luminous Mysteries or the Mysteries of Light.

With the inclusion of the five new mysteries to the Rosary in *Rosarium Virginis Mariae*, the first addition in many centuries takes place. These Luminous Myster-ies treat the public life of Christ. In summary form, the pope writes: "To recite the Rosary is nothing other than to contemplate with Mary the face of Christ" (*RVM* 3). He repeatedly emphasizes that although the Rosary is

clearly Marian in character, it is at its heart a Christo-
centric prayer.

The Rosary, now with its twenty mysteries, is in
effect a compendium of the entire gospel, a snapshot
of our faith. "It is an echo of the prayer of Mary, her
perennial *Magnificat* for the work of the redemptive
Incarnation which began in her virginal womb. With
the Rosary, the Christian people sits *at the school of Mary*
and is led to contemplate the beauty on the face of
Christ and to experience the depths of his love" (*RVM* 1).

You may have had a similar experience when praying the Rosary as I have—a deep sense of consolation.
"Many who say the Rosary think of the words as back-
ground music that leads them to rest in the divine presence. The gentle repetition of the words helps us to
enter the silence of our hearts, where Christ's Spirit
dwells" (*USCCA* 300).

So often I have experienced as well a sense of
Mary's maternal presence. She is, after all, Mother of
Christ, Mother of the Church, and our Mother. It is as
if Our Lady were praying with us each of the decades
of the Rosary. Our faith teaches us that Mary intercedes for us, as do all the saints. And Mary is Queen
of the Saints. She has a place of preeminence among
those holy men and women who have gone before us
in faith.

In each of the mysteries—the Joyful, Sorrowful, Glorious, and now the Luminous Mysteries—her
wonderful presence is felt. In each of them, Mary has
memories of her Son. "In a way those memories were
to be the 'Rosary' which she recited uninterruptedly
throughout her earthly life," a living Rosary of sorts
(*RVM* 11). As such, "in the recitation of the Rosary,

the Christian community enters into contact with the memories and the contemplative gaze of Mary" (*RVM* 11). Moreover, "the Rosary mystically transports us to Mary's side as she is busy watching over the human growth of Christ in the home of Nazareth. This enables her to train us and to mold us with the same care, until Christ is 'fully formed' in us (cf. Gal 4:19)" (*RVM* 15).

As we grow in our knowledge of the Lord Jesus, we are turned more and more to him in prayer. "If Jesus, the one Mediator, is the Way of our prayer, then Mary, his purest and most transparent reflection, shows us the Way. . . . She intercedes for us before the Father who filled her with grace and before the Son born of her womb, praying with and for us" (*RVM* 16).

The Five New Mysteries

In this chapter, our attention turns to the five Luminous Mysteries. It is an effort to incorporate these five new mysteries of Jesus' public life into the life of the Church, linking them to the present and our own spiritual life with him.

The Baptism of the Lord

The first Mystery of Light is the Baptism of the Lord. As Christ descends into the waters of the Jordan, and the Spirit descends upon him, the heavens open up and we hear the voice of the Father declaring that Jesus is his beloved Son. Jesus is identified by his heavenly Father as his beloved Son on whom his favor rests. Pope Benedict XVI writes in the first chapter of his book *Jesus of Nazareth: From the Baptism in the Jordan to the Transfiguration*:

> Jesus' Baptism anticipated his death on the cross, and the heavenly voice proclaimed an anticipation of the Resurrection. These anticipations have now become reality. . . . To accept the invitation to be baptized now means to go to the place of Jesus' Baptism. It is to go where he identifies himself with us and to receive our identification with him. The point where he anticipates death has now become the point where we anticipate rising again with him.

You and I also become children of the Father as we are washed clean at our baptisms, as many are on the vigil of Easter each year, and week in and week out at parish churches everywhere. We become children of the light from that moment.

The Miracle at Cana

The second Mystery of Light is the miracle at the wedding feast of Cana, the first of Jesus' many miracles when water was changed into wine. Mary intervenes that night, at a wedding feast, telling the waiters to do whatever Jesus tells them to do. You know the story. Cana not only implies the importance of marriage as a sacrament, as it was the first of his miracles, but it also underscores the power of Mary's intercession. The same mother of Jesus powerfully intervenes for us in our day each time we turn to her in prayer, especially as we pray the Rosary, her prayer.

The Proclamation of the Kingdom of God

The third Mystery of Light contains the first public words of Jesus, the inauguration of his mission—"This is the time of fulfillment. The kingdom of God is at hand. Repent, and believe in the gospel" (Mk 1:15). Each time we humbly repent of our sins, we experience the light piercing through the darkness of evil.

Darkness and light are constant themes in our theological lexicon. Archbishop John Quinn, the archbishop emeritus of San Francisco, spoke in Houston, Texas, to the National Federation of Priests' Councils on April 13, 2010, and said perceptively:

> And so, in a difficult time we should not forget that the great works of God have been accomplished in darkness. The people fled Egypt in the darkness; they crossed the Red Sea in the darkness; the Lord Jesus was born in Bethlehem in the darkness of night; he gave us the Eucharist and the priesthood in the darkness of the Last Supper; he died on the Cross when the Gospel says "darkness covered the earth." He lay in the darkness of the tomb. On the third day, he rose again in the darkness, and the empty tomb was discovered "early in the morning while it was still dark." God is at work even in the darkness.

In my Ash Wednesday homily this year, I focused on this third mystery of light and the need for repentance. I highlighted the call to conversion and the challenge to see light amidst the darkness of our sin. Precisely in repentance, we come to light and experience his loving embrace as the evil of our sins is forgiven. St. Jerome reminds us: "For the Lord is *gracious and merciful* and prefers conversion of a sinner rather than his death. Patient and generous in his mercy, he does not give in to human impatience but is willing to wait a long time for our repentance."

The Transfiguration

The next to the last Mystery of Light is called by our late Holy Father "the mystery of light par excellence." It is the Transfiguration of the Lord believed to have taken place high on a mountain called Mount Tabor. Many pilgrims have walked up to its peak as I did once on a pilgrimage to the Holy Land. A mountain traditionally represents the place of prayer. It reminds us, as he was transfigured in glory, of that Advent preface which reads: "It is by his gift that already we rejoice at the mystery of his Nativity, so that he may find us watchful in prayer and exultant in his praise." How else can we "listen to him" heeding the Father's words given at the moment of the Transfiguration except by persevering in daily prayer, especially the contemplative prayer of the Rosary? With the advance of social networking and all forms of media, it is increasingly difficult to be still in prayer and alone with our God. There seems to be a constant need to be distracted or entertained. The sheer volume of information seems to crowd out our capacity for contemplation and prayer. It makes it more difficult to heed the voice of the Father at the Transfiguration, a voice that encourages us to "listen" to his Son.

The Institution of the Eucharist

And finally, the last Mystery of Light is the Institution of the Eucharist. Repeatedly called the "source and summit" of our lives as Catholics, it is the Eucharist in which Christ offers his body and blood as food under the signs of bread and wine. Could there be a more profound mystery of light?

I spoke of this new fifth mystery of the Rosary in my homily on Holy Thursday, the night of its institution. There is never enough time to contemplate fully the face of the Eucharistic Christ, for the Eucharist is truly a great mystery, a Mystery of Light, a mystery of mercy, a mystery of redeeming and transforming love, an unsurpassable gift. The Eucharist is both gift *and* mystery!

Blessed John Paul II wrote of this in his encyclical *Church of the Eucharist (Ecclesia de Eucharistia)*:

> The Church constantly draws her life from [his] redeeming sacrifice; she approaches it not only through faith-filled remembrance, but also through *a real contact, since this sacrifice is made present ever anew, sacramentally perpetuated,* in every community which offers it at the hands of the consecrated minister. . . . What is repeated is its memorial

> celebration . . . which makes Christ's one,
> definitive redemptive sacrifice always
> present in time. (*EDE* 12)

Even the place of his birth, the city of Bethlehem, means "House of Bread." We have become heirs to the most holy Eucharist, the bread of eternal life.

Taken together, the twenty mysteries of the Rosary are akin to a compendium of the entire gospel with the five new mysteries giving us a snapshot of the public life of Jesus.

A Meditation

I would like to add some personal points for your reflection, hopefully to help you as you meditate on the five new mysteries. These are a result of my own prayer and a conviction I received a few summers ago in Italy as I was praying at the tomb of the true apostle of the Rosary, Blessed Bartolo Longo, the nineteenth-century lawyer greatly responsible for the construction of the Basilica of Our Lady of the Rosary in Pompeii.

In each of these mysteries, in my prayer in that basilica as I was praying the Mysteries of Light, I was struck by a voice and a sacrament. Briefly, here is my reflection:

The Baptism of the Lord

It is the voice of the Father: "This is my beloved Son, with whom I am well pleased" (Mt 3:17). Reflect on your own Baptism and the importance Baptism is in our individual lives as followers of Jesus, how we share in the priestly, prophetic and royal mission of Jesus precisely because of our Baptism.

The Miracle at Cana

It is the voice of Mary: "Do whatever he tells you" (Jn 2:5). Reflect on Mary's intercessory power, and the importance of marriage in the Christian life, and the first public miracle of Jesus.

The Proclamation of the Kingdom of God

It is the voice of Jesus, his first public words: "This is the time of fulfillment. The kingdom of God is at hand. Repent, and believe in the gospel" (Mk 1:15). Reflect on the integral importance of repentance in our lives and the link to faith. An examined life is fundamental to our following Christ, as are the healing sacraments of Penance and the Anointing of the Sick.

The Transfiguration

It is the voice of the Father: "This is my beloved Son. Listen to him" (Mk 9:7). With the cloud and the representatives of the law and prophets, we think of the Holy Spirit and Confirmation. His disciples were confirmed in their faith as they continued their journey to Jerusalem. As we ponder the law and prophetic voice of Jesus and the prophets, we are continually confirmed in our faith. The Father also exhorts us to pray. "Listen to him."

The Institution of the Eucharist

It is the voice of Jesus, "Do this in memory of me" (Lk 22:19). Reflect on the gift of the Eucharist, its fundamental importance in our lives, and on the Sacrament of Holy Orders.

These five new mysteries of the Rosary form the basis of a type of spirituality. In each one, I invite you to listen prayerfully and carefully to the voice and in addition to focus on the sacrament it reflects. The sacraments, after all, are concrete ways in which the public ministry of Jesus continues in our day and in every age in and through you and me. They are transforming encounters with Christ.

A Witness to Prayer

Prayer has been a central part of my life for the past twenty years. I begin each day by reading the Bible, in which I have found, God speaks to us. Praying is our way in which we attempt to speak to God and the final part of this special communication is for us to take time for reflection, in which we can hopefully allow God's word to be absorbed by us and his voice to be heard. This time in the morning is my "first fruit" of the day, but it is often a struggle to resist the typical distractions of pending to do lists or the gravitational pull to check e-mail first. My best time of the day or the week is when I can push through these distractions and allow Christ to have this time with me, just him, his word and his time. Over the years, I have grown to spend the vast majority of that morning prayer time with intercessory prayers for those closest to me in my life, as well as others I have come across who really need God's help and direction in their lives.

At the end of each day before I get into bed, I attempt to reconnect with my prayer life with God much like we did as children with our parents when we remember their guiding us in saying, "Now I lay me down to sleep. . . ." However as an adult, I now review the events of the day, the times when I felt God's grace and blessings and thank Him for those. At the same time, I also acknowledge yet another day when I know I disappointed God but pray for another chance to try to do a better job and get it right the next day.

—John G. Shooshan

Reflect

1. What place does the Rosary play in your life? What is your experience when you pray the Rosary?

2. What are some of the times and situations in which you or others you know have found praying the Rosary to be helpful?

3. Besides the Rosary, are there other Marian devotions that are helpful to you? In what ways are they helpful?

Pray

Blessed John Paul II concluded his apostolic letter, *The Rosary of the Virgin Mary* with this prayer.

Supplication to the Queen of the Holy Rosary

O Blessed Rosary of Mary, sweet chain which unites us to God, bond of love which unites us to the angels, tower of salvation against the assaults of Hell, safe port in our universal shipwreck, we will never abandon you. You will be our comfort in the hour of death: yours our final kiss as life ebbs away. And the last word from our lips will be your sweet name, O Queen of the Rosary of Pompeii, O dearest Mother, O Refuge of Sinners, O Sovereign Consoler of the Afflicted. May you be everywhere blessed, today and always, on earth and in heaven. (*RVM* 43)

—Blessed Bartolo Longo
The Apostle of the Rosary

nine

The Our Father

The Our Father is at once the prayer of God, and in the words of Tertullian, "truly the summary of the whole gospel." It is a prayer in response to the request of Jesus' disciple who asked him simply, "Lord, teach us to pray." How grateful we should be to that one disciple who made that request. He must have asked him because they were so impressed with Jesus' own prayer life. It was prayer addressed to his Father. We are forever indebted to him for asking Jesus that question and for the answer Jesus gave us.

As Pope Benedict writes: "The meaning of the Our Father goes much further than the mere provision of a prayer text. It aims to form our being, to train us in the inner attitude of Jesus" (cf. Phil 2:5). This inner attitude reflects his prayerful dialogue with his Father.

What about us? How often do we ask the Lord Jesus that same question with respect to how we should pray? How often, moreover, do we make requests of the Lord—specific requests regarding our health, our job, our family, or the health, jobs, and families of others who are close to us? Most of the time, many of these prayers of petition are really based on the prayer Jesus gave us. And that is the prayer entitled simply the Our Father. It is *the* fundamental Christian prayer. When we think about it, the Our Father has a *central* place in the scripture, in our worship, and in our lives as Christians and Catholics. It has always had a place of importance from the very beginning since it is the prayer Jesus gave us. But is it central to our prayer lives?

St. Augustine once wrote: "Run through all the words of the holy prayers [in Scripture] and I do not think that you will find anything in them that is not contained and included in the Lord's Prayer" (CCC 2762). The Our Father can be found both in the Gospel of St. Matthew and St. Luke. Matthew's version (which is the one the Church has adopted) is the central part of the Sermon on the Mount (Mt 6:9–13). Luke's version, a gospel often referred to as the "gospel of prayer," can be found in what is referred to as the Sermon on the Plain (Lk 11:2–4). This prayer was so important that the early Church Fathers—Augustine, Tertullian, Cyprian—wrote sermons and essays on it. The sermons were often addressed to the catechumens and neophytes. St. Thomas Aquinas referred to the Our Father as "the most perfect of prayers" (CCC 2763).

To underscore again the centrality of this prayer, the Catechism teaches us that it is the "quintessential prayer of the Church. It is an integral part of the major hours of the Divine Office and of the sacraments of Christian initiation: Baptism, Confirmation, and the Eucharist" (CCC 2776). At each Mass, before Holy Communion, we recite the Our Father together. "In the *Eucharistic liturgy* the Lord's Prayer appears as the prayer of the whole Church and there reveals its full meaning and efficacy" (CCC 2770). We pray the Our Father over and over again in the Rosary as well. The early Christians prayed it three times each day.

The centrality of the Our Father really should not surprise us. After all, it is "the prayer to our Father . . . taught and given to us by the Lord Jesus. The prayer that comes to us from Jesus is truly unique: it is 'of the Lord'" (*CCC* 2765). The Our Father is an "indivisible gift of the Lord's words and of the Holy Spirit who gives life to them in the hearts of believers" (*CCC* 2767).

The Our Father contains seven petitions. The first three deal with God. The last four concern us. The relationship of the two sets of petitions could be compared to the relationship between the two tablets of the Ten Commandments—the first three refer to God and the last seven refer to one's neighbor. Before we examine more closely the seven petitions, however, we start with the addressee of this prayer that Jesus taught us. It is the Father—his Father, our Father.

Abba

Our Father

Father in Aramaic, *abba*, has to be one of the most important words in the entire Bible. The best translation is "daddy" or "daddy dear." Consider how radical this was for the Jewish mind—to call God daddy. What intimacy! What familial closeness! It is a far cry from God speaking to Moses from the burning bush where God told him: "Do not come near; put off your shoes from your feet, for the place on which you are standing is holy ground" (*CCC* 2777).

Pope Benedict writes:

> It is true, of course, that contemporary
> men and women have difficulty experi-
> encing the great consolation of the word
> *father* immediately, since the experience
> of the father is in many cases either com-
> pletely absent or is obscured by inade-
> quate examples of fatherhood.

We must thus allow Jesus, the Eternal Son, to
teach us what *father* really means and how it is that
we can call God "Abba, daddy dear." As we grow in
our relationship with his Son, Jesus, we become more
clearly aware of our relationship as sons and daughters to his Father. He thus becomes more and more a
personal God. At its heart, however, "we can invoke
God as 'Father' because *he is revealed to us* by his Son
. . . and because his Spirit makes him known to us"
(*CCC* 2780).

Not only does Jesus teach us about *the Father*. In
this prayer, he teaches us about *ourselves*. By Baptism, we become adopted sons and daughters of the
Father. With Jesus, each one of us is empowered by the
Holy Spirit to call God "Abba." But as Pope Benedict
reminds us in his analysis of the Our Father: "The Our
Father is always a prayer of Jesus and that communion
with him is what opens it up for us." Moreover, "the
personal relation of the Son to the Father is something
that man cannot conceive of nor the angelic powers
even dimly see: and yet, the Spirit of the Son grants
a participation in that very relation to us who believe
that Jesus is the Christ and that we are born of God"
(*CCC* 2780). Praying to the Father should develop in us

the will to become like him and foster in us a humble and trusting heart (*CCC* 2800).

Not only do we call God Father but we also importantly refer to him as *Our* Father. "The adjective, as used by us, does not express possession, but an entirely new relationship with God" (*CCC* 2786). That relationship affects our relationship to each other. By Baptism, we belong to each other. As Archbishop Thomas Collins writes:

> We are not little islands, separate from one another. We are brothers and sisters in the Lord, part of the family of faith, into which we enter through baptism. We always live in the reality of the community of the disciples of Jesus, "Our Father." So we cannot pray, "My Father," and forget our brothers and sisters. This community is always with us, to the end of time when we will be in the heavenly Jerusalem.

Admittedly, however, we live in a community with a strong emphasis on individualism. When we pray Our Father, we are challenged to leave that individualism aside and to exclude no one. Not only is the Father close to us in prayer. We are close to each other, those other adopted sons and daughters, as we pray.

Who art in heaven

St. Augustine explained this expression so well when he wrote:

> "Our Father who art in heaven" is right-
> ly understood to mean that God is in the
> hearts of the just, as in his holy temple.
> At the same time, it means that those
> who pray should desire the one they
> invoke to dwell in them. (*CCC* 2794)

So understood, heaven is not a place beyond the stars, but a way of being. God, although majestic, lives within us and we live in him. When we pray in this way, we ask for a more profound experience of the presence of God within us right now. Is that not the essence of prayer?

"After we have placed ourselves in the presence of God our Father . . . the Spirit . . . stirs up in our hearts seven petitions, seven blessings" (*CCC* 2803). The first three petitions—name, kingdom, will—move us to God. The second four petitions are about bread, trespasses, temptation, and the Evil One. They help us focus on our basic needs, our needs of feeding, heal-ing, battling for victory of life and protection. We now reflect on them one by one.

Three Petitions to God

Hallowed be thy name

In the biblical sense, a person's name is synony-mous with that very person. A name expresses and manifests who a person is. The term *hallow* means "to recognize as holy, to treat in a holy way" (*CCC* 2807). Hence when we pray "hallowed be thy name," we are praying that we might continue to recognize the very person of God as holy, as set apart, as worthy of our praise and adoration. "The holiness of God is the inaccessible center of his eternal mystery" (CCC 2809).

St. Cyprian, commenting on the Our Father, wrote:

> By whom is God hallowed, since he is the one who hallows? But since he said, "You shall be holy to me; for I the Lord am holy," we seek and ask that we who were sanctified in Baptism may persevere in what we have begun to be. And we ask this daily, for we need sanctification daily, so that we who fail daily may cleanse away our sins by being sanctified continually. . . . We pray that this sanctification may remain in us. (CCC 2813)

In praying that God's holiness, his presence, might always be foremost in our lives, we also pray that he might keep us holy and close to him. In the end, moreover, it is primarily God who makes holy his name. At the Last Supper, Jesus prayed: "Holy Father, protect in your name those whom you have given me" (Jn 17:11). He was praying for you and me as he teaches us to make holy the name of God the Father, "daddy dear." How do I treat his holy name?

Thy kingdom come

The kingdom of God is in effect the breaking through into our world of the presence of Jesus Christ. When we pray "thy kingdom come," we pray that we might experience more deeply the person of Jesus in our lives both *now* and *at his final coming*. In effect, the kingdom is already here on earth, but not fully here "since Christ's final transformation of individuals, society, and culture has yet to happen in its fullness. This is why we need to pray this petition every day and work for its coming" (*USCCA* 486). Romans 14:17 teaches us that "the kingdom of God is not a matter of food and drink, but of justice, peace and joy in the Holy Spirit." Hence when we pray for God's kingdom to be made manifest in our day, we pray that we in our own way may push the world to be more just, peaceful, and joyful. This all takes place in the power of the Holy Spirit. It is what we pray for in this second petition. The Catechism teaches: "Since Pentecost, the coming of that reign is the work of the Spirit of the Lord who 'completes his work on earth and brings us the fullness of grace'" (*CCC* 2818).

> By a discernment according to the Spirit, Christians have to distinguish between the growth of the Reign of God and the progress of the culture and society in which they are involved. This distinction is not a separation. Man's vocation to eternal life does not suppress, but actually reinforces, his duty to put into action in this world the energies and means received from the Creator to serve justice and peace. (*CCC* 2820)

Thy will be done on earth as it is in heaven

Jesus took this petition to heart in his earthly life. He expects us likewise to make it a significant part of our prayer life. The night before Jesus died, during the agony in the Garden of Gethsemane, he prayed: "Father, if you are willing, take this cup away from me; still, not my will but your will be done" (Lk 22:42). Here Jesus consents totally to the will of his Father even unto death. In his study of the Our Father, Pope Benedict instructs us that when we pray this third petition, "We are asking that the drama of the Mount of Olives, the struggle of Jesus' entire life and work, be brought to completion in us; that together with him, the Son, we may unite our wills with the Father's will, thus becoming sons in our turn. . . ."

In this prayerful petition, "we ask our Father to unite our will to his Son's, in order to fulfill his will, his plan of salvation for the life of the world" (CCC 2825). The love command, love one another as I have loved you, "summarizes all the others [commandments] and expresses his entire will" (CCC 2822). That is our daily challenge. And it should be at the heart of our prayer lives, that we love each other as Jesus did, always putting the other person first and giving our lives and hearts for another if need be. That is the will of God for us.

Standing alone, "we are radically incapable of this, but united with Jesus and with the power of his Holy Spirit, we can surrender our will to him and decide to choose what his Son has always chosen: to do what is pleasing to the Father" (CCC 2825). That should give us reassurance every time we pray "thy will be done," not mine. Moreover, "by prayer we can discern 'what is the will of God' and obtain the endurance to do it. Jesus teaches us that one enters the kingdom of heaven not by speaking words, but by doing 'the will of my Father in heaven'" (*CCC* 2826). It means action over words, and love above all.

Petitions for Our Needs

Give us this day our daily bread

With this fourth petition, we turn to God, prayerfully asking that he care for us and that in turn we care for each other. This is so countercultural because each of us likes to live under the illusion that we are self-sufficient and that everyone else should be also. "'Give us': The trust of children who look to their Father for everything is beautiful" (*CCC* 2828). In this petition, we seek, in the power of the Holy Spirit, to develop a trusting relationship to God who is our daddy. "Give us *this* day," which means one day at a time. Prayerfully we should not be worrying about tomorrow. Our focus is *this* day, *this* hour, *this* moment. Give us now, O Lord, in effect means: what we need and nothing more but only what we presently need for our nourishment.

There is a social justice theme here as well. The Catechism teaches:

> The presence of those who hunger because they lack bread opens up another profound meaning of this petition. The drama of hunger in the world calls Christians who pray sincerely to

exercise responsibility toward their brethren, both in their personal behavior and in their solidarity with the human family. This petition of the Lord's Prayer cannot be isolated from the parables of the poor man Lazarus and of the Last Judgment. (CCC 2831)

"'Our' bread is the 'one' loaf for the 'many'" (CCC 2833). In praying for our daily bread, we pray for the generosity of heart to share our bread with others.

Now there is another part of this petition. We pray "Give us this day" and then we add immediately "our daily bread." We learn from Origen that the word *daily* (*epiousios*) appears nowhere else in the Greek New Testament. Taken literally, it means "super-essential." This has been understood to mean the "super-essential" bread which is the Bread of Life, the Body of Christ, the medicine of immortality without which we have no life within us. After all, "man does not live by bread alone, but . . . by every word that proceeds from the mouth of God" (Mt 4:4). And that word is the Word of God. It is Jesus, the Word Incarnate, which is his Body and Blood. We pray in this petition not only for our material needs but importantly for our spiritual "bread," for regular reception of the Eucharist and the grace to see in the Eucharist the great saving food for our salvation.

And forgive us our trespasses as we forgive those who trespass against us

In this most important petition, we acknowledge that we are sinners, that we are trespassers not unlike the prodigal son or the tax collector who confessed they were sinners. Oh what an important acknowledgment in the life of a Christian, of every Catholic! With this petition, we not only take ownership of our sins but pray for forgiveness and pray for the grace to forgive those who sin against us. We pray for the grace to receive the sacrament of Penance often and to experience the mercy of God, which is beyond all telling. And we are reminded of the exhortation of St. Paul to the Ephesians: "Get rid of all bitterness, all passion and anger, harsh words, slander, and malice of every kind. In place of these, be kind to one another, compassionate, and mutually forgiving, just as God has forgiven you in Christ" (Eph 4:31–32).

Jesus took this petition to heart even on the wood of the cross: "Father, forgive them for they know not what they do" (Lk 23:24). Christ died that "sins might be forgiven." At its core, then, this petition for forgiveness challenges us to be like Christ himself. "It reminds us," writes Pope Benedict, "of he who allowed forgiveness to cost him descent into the hardship of human existence and death on the Cross."

We pray for forgiveness. This is a theme that permeates the entire gospel. And we pray also that we be empowered to "forgive those who trespass against us." Forgiveness from the heart is often very difficult. Alone it is impossible to forgive. The Catechism reminds us: "There has to be a vital participation, coming from the depths of the heart, in the holiness and the mercy and the love of our God. Only the Spirit by whom we live can make 'ours' the same mind that was in Christ Jesus" (CCC 2842). That is our prayer.

And lead us not into temptation

"When we say 'lead us not into temptation,' we are asking God not to allow us to take the path that leads to sin. This petition implores the Spirit of discernment and strength; it requires the grace of vigilance and final perseverance" (*CCC* 2863). Archbishop Collins notes that it is important to realize: "Temptation is not a sin. It's a testing. If we fail in the test—if when probed by the situation we then consent to evil—then that is a sin. . . . The testing is part of the condition of our journey."

In our family and work lives, we are continually challenged between good and evil and between right and wrong. "We are engaged in the battle 'between flesh and spirit'" (*CCC* 2846). Choosing good, the right, and the Spirit is only possible through prayer. In fact Jesus prayed for us to the Father at the Last Supper when he said: "Keep them in your name" (Jn 17:11). The Letter to the Hebrews, speaking of Jesus, reminds us: "Because he himself was tested through what he suffered, he is able to help those who are being tested" (Heb 2:18).

Through prayer and in the power of the Holy Spirit we too can "discern between trials, which are necessary for the growth of the inner man, and temptation, which leads to sin and death" (*CCC* 2847). This is at the heart of the sixth petition.

But deliver us from evil

The Catechism makes it clear that evil is a person in the world. So often this is the butt of jokes as is the existence of hell. But it is our faith. "The evil we confront is not just an abstract idea, but an evil, fallen angel who wants to prevent our salvation" (*USCCA* 489).

"In the last petition, 'but deliver us from evil,' Christians pray to God with the Church to show forth the victory, already won by Christ, over the 'ruler of this world,' Satan, the angel personally opposed to God and to his plan of salvation" (*CCC* 2864). Jesus prayed this same prayer at the Last Supper: "I do not ask that you take them out of the world but that you keep them from the evil one" (Jn 17:15).

As if to summarize this final petition of the Our Father, we look to the text from the Roman Missal prayed at Mass after the Our Father: "Deliver us, Lord, we pray, from every evil, graciously grant peace in our days, that, by the help of your mercy, we may be always free from sin and safe from all distress, as we await the blessed hope and the coming of our Savior, Jesus Christ."

Amen.

At the end of the prayer, we say Amen. It is another way of saying: "So be it."

A Witness to Prayer

"An unexamined life is not worth living" (Socrates). The Examen Prayer of St. Ignatius of Loyola is a simple prayer that has become the cornerstone of my personal prayer life. The Examen allows one to become more aware of God's presence in his life and gives him the understanding to take action in response to God's presence. Ten to thirty minutes of daily silent prayer goes a long way, especially when we ask for the Good Lord's active participation through these three easy steps: (1) becoming aware, (2) understanding, and (3) taking action. By prayerfully reviewing the last twenty-four hours of our life, we (1) become aware of those times or experiences when we were either close to or far from God. By spending time revisiting and discerning these experiences, we (2) move beyond feelings and emotions to the origin of these experiences and begin to understand why we experience them. Lastly, with this greater understanding of ourselves and the good and evil spirits at work within us, we (3) take the appropriate action to move closer to God by rejecting that which is not from him and embracing what he desires to give us.

"If we could lift the veil and if we watched with vigilant attention, God would endlessly reveal himself to us and we should see and rejoice in his active presence in all that befalls us. At every event we should exclaim: 'It is the Lord!'" (Jean Pierre de Caussade)

—Rev. Mark Ivany

Reflect

1. When do you pray the Our Father? How much is it a part of your prayer life?

2. What new insights did you gain about any of the petitions of the Our Father?

Pray

I wish to conclude this book on prayer with the words of St. Anselm from his *Proslogion*. These are words that should help each of us in our daily efforts at communion with our God. St. Anselm writes:

Teach me to seek you, and when I seek you show yourself to me, for I cannot seek you unless you teach me, nor can I find you unless you show yourself to me. Let me seek you in desiring you and desire you in seeking you, find you in loving you and love you in finding you.

Abbreviations

EDE *Church of the Eucharist (Ecclesia de Eucharistia).* Encyclical of Blessed John Paul II, 2003.

EN *Evangelization in the Modern World (Evangelii Nuntiandi).* Apostolic Exhortation of Pope Paul VI, 1975.

DCE *God Is Love (Deus Caritas Est).* Encyclical of Pope Benedict XVI, 2006.

SC *Constitution on the Sacred Liturgy (Sacrosanctum Concilium).* Vatican Council II, 1963.

SD *On the Christian Meaning of Human Suffering (Salvifici Doloris)* Apostolic Letter of Blessed John Paul II, 1984.

VD *The Word of the Lord (Verbum Domini).* Post-Synodal Apostolic Exhortation. Pope Benedict XVI, 2011.

RVM *Rosary of the Virgin Mary (Rosarium Virginis Mariae).* Apostolic Letter of Blessed John Paul II, 2002.

VS *The Splendor of Truth (Veritatis Splendor)* Encyclical Letter of Blessed John Paul II, 1993.

References

Introduction

Gerald O'Collins, S.J., *Pause for Thought: Making Time for Prayer, Jesus, and God* (Mahwah, NJ: Paulist Press, 2011), 15.

Chapter 1. Prayer, God's Gift and Initiative in Our Lives

Peter Turkson as quoted in James Roberts, "Mission Possible," *The Tablet,* August 1, 2009, www.thetablet .co.uk/issue/1000167.

John Chrysostom, Supp., Hom. 6 *De precatione, PG* 64:462–466, as quoted in *Liturgy of the Hours,* Friday after Ash Wednesday.

Chapter 2. Old Testament Models of Prayer

Pope St. Pius X, from the Apostolic Constitution *Divino afflatu,* as quoted in *Liturgy of the Hours,* memorial of Pius X, August 21.

Lawrence S. Cunningham, "Praying the Psalms: Some Notes," *America,* August 2, 1997, 8.

Chapter 3. Jesus, the Master of Prayer

Theological Historical Commission for the Great Jubilee Year 2000, *Jesus Christ: Word of the Father,* (New York: Crossroad Publishing, 1997), 131.

Ibid., 134.

Chapter 4. Prayer in the Life of the Church

Thomas Collins, *Pathway to our Hearts* (Notre Dame, IN: Ave Maria Press, 2011), xv.

Jem Sullivan, *The Beauty of Faith* (Huntington, IN: Our Sunday Visitor, 2009), 36–37.

Donald Cardinal Wuerl, *The Mass* (New York: Doubleday, 2011), 148.

John Paul II, *Crossing the Threshold of Hope* (New York: Alfred A. Knopf, 1994), 19.

Louis de Montfort, *True Devotion to the Blessed Virgin* (Langley Bucks, England: St. Paul Publications, 1962), 182.

Augustine DiNoia, *The Love That Never Ends* (Huntington, IN: Our Sunday Visitor, 1996), 140.

Louis de Montfort, 184, 185.

Chapter 5. The Practicalities of Prayer

Jean Vianney, *"Catéchisme sur la prière"* in A. Monnin, *Esprit du Curé d'Ars* (Paris, 1899) as quoted in *Liturgy of the Hours*, August 4.

Dorothy Day, *Thérèse* (Springfield, IL: Templegate, 1960), 160.

Augustine, "Letter to Proba" as quoted in *Liturgy of the Hours*, Twenty-Ninth Sunday of Ordinary Time.

Robert F. Morneau, *Paths to Prayer* (Cincinnati: St. Anthony Messenger Press, 1998), 19.

Chapter 6. The Prayer of Jesus on Holy Thursday

Pope Benedict XVI, *Jesus of Nazareth, Holy Week: From the Entrance into Jerusalem to the Resurrection* (San Francisco: Ignatius Press, 2011), 156.

Thomas More, *The Sadness of Christ* (New York: Scepter Publishing, 1993) 32, 23.

Chapter 7. The Prayer of Jesus from the Cross

Pope Benedict XVI, *Jesus of Nazareth* (2011), 211–12.

Ibid., 208.

Alfred McBride, O. Praem., *The Seven Last Words of Jesus* (Cincinnati: St. Anthony Messenger Press, 1990).

Romanus Cessario, O.P., *The Seven Last Words of Jesus* (San Francisco: Ignatius Press, 2009).

Fulton J. Sheen, *The Seven Last Words* (New York: Alba House, 1995).

Romanus Cessario, 17.

Fulton J. Sheen, 18.

Pope Benedict XVI, *Jesus of Nazareth* (2011), 214.

Ibid., 214.

Romanus Cessario, 44.

Alfred McBride, 54.

Fulton J. Sheen, 51–52.

Alfred McBride, 68.

Chapter 8. The Rosary

Pope Benedict XVI, *Jesus of Nazareth: From the Baptism in the Jordan to the Transfiguration* (New York: Doubleday, 2007), 18.

Jerome, A commentary on Joel, as quoted in *Liturgy of the Hours*, Friday, Twenty-First Week in Ordinary Time.

John Quinn, "Do Not Despair," *America*, May 3, 2010. Accessed August 23, 2011. http://www.americamagazine.org/content/article.cfm?article_id=12258.

Chapter 9. The Our Father

Pope Benedict XVI, *Jesus of Nazareth* (2007), 132.

Ibid., 136.

Ibid., 135.

Thomas Collins, 71.

Pope Benedict XVI, *Jesus of Nazareth* (2007), 341.

Ibid., 160.

Thomas Collins, 79.

Anselm, *Proslogion*. Cap. 1: Opera Omnia edited by Schmit, Secovii, 1938, 1:97–100 as quoted in *Liturgy of the Hours*, Friday, First Week of Advent.

Msgr. Peter J. Vaghi is pastor of the Church of the Little Flower in Bethesda, Maryland, and a priest of the Archdiocese of Washington. He received seminary and theological training at the Pontifical North American College and Gregorian University, both in Rome. Also a graduate of University of Virginia Law School, Vaghi practiced law for many years and remains a member of the Virginia State Bar and the District of Columbia Bar. Vaghi serves as chaplain to the John Carroll Society, a group of professional men and women in service of the Archbishop of Washington. He is the author of the Pillars of Faith series—*The Faith We Profess, The Sacraments We Celebrate, The Commandments We Keep,* and *The Prayer We Offer*—and has written a number of articles for *America, Priest,* and *Our Sunday Visitor.* He has also contributed to two collections of writings on priestly spirituality: *Behold Your Mother* and *Born of the Eucharist.*

Founded in 1865, Ave Maria Press,
a ministry of the Congregation of
Holy Cross, is a Catholic publishing
company that serves the spiritual and
formative needs of the Church and its
schools, institutions, and ministers;
Christian individuals and families; and
others seeking spiritual nourishment.

For a complete listing of titles from

Ave Maria Press

Sorin Books

Forest of Peace

Christian Classics

visit www.avemariapress.com

 ave maria press® / Notre Dame, IN 46556
A Ministry of the United States Province of Holy Cross